Conflict Resolution and De-Escalation Strategies

Conflict Resolution and De-Escalation Strategies

LASERIAN UGOH

Conflict Resolution And De-Escalation Strategies
Copyright © 2021 by Laserian Ugoh. All rights reserved.

No part of this publication may be reproduced, stored in a retrieval system or transmitted in any way by any means, electronic, mechanical, photocopy, recording or otherwise without the prior permission of the author except as provided by USA copyright law.

The opinions expressed by the author are not necessarily those of URLink Print and Media.

1603 Capitol Ave., Suite 310 Cheyenne, Wyoming USA 82001
1-888-980-6523 | admin@urlinkpublishing.com

URLink Print and Media is committed to excellence in the publishing industry.

Book design copyright © 2021 by URLink Print and Media. All rights reserved.

Published in the United States of America

Library of Congress Control Number: 2021905379
ISBN 978-1-64753-738-8 (Paperback)
ISBN 978-1-64753-739-5 (Digital)

04.03.21

CONTENTS

Introduction 9

I

Antecedents Of Conflict Resolution 11
   Relevant Terminology

II

Mediation 17
   Mediation Process
   Mediator Styles

III

Factors Influencing Mediation 29
   Mediation And Culture
   Mediation And Language
   Mediation and Power Balance

IV

Mediation Techniques 45
   - Going To The Balcony
   - Step To Their Side & Reframe
   - Building A Bridge
   - Power To Educate
   - Turning Adversaries into Partners

V

Psychological Legitimacy Of Mediation 57
   Logotherapy
   Crisis Intervention
   Conflict Management
   Conflict Prevention
   Conflict Transformation

VI

Terrorism 71
    Injustice
    Frustration
    Jealousy
    Fanaticism
    Intimidation

VII

Religion, Spirituality And Mediation 89
    The Islamic Faith

VIII

Revolution And Conflict De-Escalation 102
    The Arab Spring And Conflict De-Escalation

IX

Conflict Resolution And Leadership 122
    Martin Luther King, Jr.
    Nelson Mandela
    Mohandas Gandhi
    Aristotle
    Christopher Columbus
    Charles Schwab
    Robert Mugabe
    Napoleon Bonaparte
    Augustus Caesar
    Napoleon Bonaparte And Augustus Caesar
    Adolf Hitler
    Joseph Stalin
    Adolf Hitler And Joseph Stalin
    Leadership Styles

X

Mediation And Cultural Types 146
    Western
    South & Central American
    Central European
    Eastern European
    Middle Eastern
    African
    Asian

XI

Conflict Resolution versus Propaganda 152

XII

Prospects Of Conflict Resolution And De-escalation 157

Conclusion 169
Epilogue 183
Resources and Bibliography 185

INTRODUCTION

"It is so easy to break down and destroy. The heroes are those who make peace and build." – Nelson Mandela.

Since its inception following the events of the Second World War, the United Nations has played vital mediation roles across the globe. Some of these mediation efforts have been so successful that issues were resolved for good. Some have not been so successful because of various reasons, ranging from the nature of the issues, to the personality of the mediators and to the mediation techniques.

Specifically, the use of mediation in conflict resolution will be one central focus of this work. This entire discourse is intended to reveal ways that a more peaceful transition stands a better chance of happening if proper mediation techniques and skilled mediators are engaged in conflict resolutions. These trained mediators must be vast in specific international, local, community, school, workplace or interpersonal mediation skills with specific regard to the languages of those involved and the historical and most salient cultural factors that influence leadership decisions.

While this is not an attempt at exhaustively providing solutions to all forms of conflicts, it will study certain origins of conflicts around the globe. The intention here is far from making this a panacea or silver bullet for settling conflicts allover the globe. Nonetheless, this study will touch on the role of mediation in addressing issues before they escalate. Even after a conflict, there is hope for reconciliation, which is made possible by proper mediation techniques.

Although it is not a study of leadership, it will discuss issues bordering on possession and wielding of power and authority. It will showcase certain notable leaders in relation to their leadership styles and contributions to world history. Some of these leaders contributed a lot to maintenance of peace and tranquility in society. On the flip side, some were only concerned with creating confusion and unrest in their time.

Note that throughout the work, there may be interchange of certain terms, such as: dispute resolution; conflict de-escalation; conflict resolution; mediation.

I
ANTECEDENTS OF CONFLICT RESOLUTION

From Harry Truman (1945) to George W. Bush (2001), virtually every American president has tried to mediate in conflicts in the Arab world. Many of these mediation efforts have produced positive results. The problem is that the resultant reprieves are often short-lived. It's not been a happy history (Tristam, 2012). Some of the resolutions last as long as the meeting ends and the negotiators return to their constituents. The intent to satisfy the people sometimes is the reason these accords are so short-lived. While the negotiators believe they have reached a consensus, their constituents may not be satisfied with such agreements. This has caused the death of leaders in the past. Many negotiators have fallen victim. Two prominent examples include Mahatma Gandhi of India and Anwar el Sadat of Egypt.

On Oct. 6, 1981, while celebrating the eighth anniversary of the 1973 war against Israel, Sadat was gunned down during the military parade. His assailants had been members of a Muslim Brotherhood breakaway group who declared him an apostate (for not imposing Sharia law in Egypt) and denounced the peace treaty with Israel (Tristam, 2012).

The purpose of mediation is bringing people together with an unbiased third party in order to settle a dispute (Schechter, 2012). Since mediation is aimed at attaining this purpose, some individuals and groups are yet to get the message right. An example is this statement credited to an influential public opinion analyst. "But we do live in a world where we can take actions in pursuit of policies that serve our national interests. For example, it would be in our interest to weaken ties between Syria and Iran" (Johnson, 2011).

As if in concert with the above writer, former United States president G.W. Bush, commenting on the interventions in the Middle East, remarked, "And if the United States tires of fighting in the streets of Baghdad, …we will face the terrorists in the streets of our own cities…So the United States will not leave until victory is achieved…" (Stout, 2006). But the big question remains whether the aim of mediation is to achieve victory against the enemy or to work together towards achieving peace in a conflict-ridden world?

In mediation, the disputants take the center stage and decide their own fate. The best resolution to a crisis is usually formulated and implemented by the disputants themselves. "The mediator's role is to facilitate communication between the parties, not to impose solutions. Mediators do not advise, take sides or render a judgment. Instead, the mediator will work with all the parties to help them reach a mutually acceptable resolution." (*Ccrchicago.org.* 2012).

This work takes another look at conflicts in general, with a view to address those areas where mediation needs to be applied to resolve seeming intractable conflicts. The watchword remains to use what obtains in a region to address the region's issues. In other words, the best successful and lasting peace is one willingly contracted by the principal actors in a dispute. Previous approaches have often succeeded in selling a tailor-made idea of conflict resolution to an entirely different culture. A quick example is the somewhat intractable and volatile conflicts in the Middle East. It could not be hyperbolic to suggest that the region would be happy to live in peace and harmony. So far, the Arab world has not known much lasting peace owing largely to external (misdirected) conflict resolution efforts. The people have been confused with a style of mediation that the west foists on them. This necessitates the presentation of options for methods of mediation that will be successful and stand the test of time in this region. It may as well serve to assist the newly Arab Spring-induced leaderships to begin a new way of resolving conflicts.

Relevant Terminology

Conflict, Crisis, Intervention, Management, Prevention, and Transformation are terms, which often resonate with conflict situations. Therefore, a definition of these terms will go a long way in helping to understand their place in mediation. Professional mediators need to understand these terms and their place in mediation to effectively practice, irrespective of the type of conflict and the region of the world involved.

Conflict: A state of open, often prolonged fighting: a battle or war. It is a state of disharmony between incompatible or antithetical persons, ideas, or interests: a clash. It could also be defined as a psychic struggle, often unconscious, resulting from the opposition or simultaneous functioning of mutually exclusive impulses, desires, or tendencies. (*TheFreeDictionary*, 2012).

Crisis: A psychological or social condition characterized by unusual instability caused by excessive stress and either endangering or felt to endanger the continuity of an individual or group; *especially*: such a social condition requiring the transformation of cultural patterns and values. (*Merriam-Webster Online Dictionary*, 2012).

Crisis Intervention refers to the methods used to offer immediate, short-term help to individuals who experience an event that produces emotional, mental, physical, and behavioral distress or problems (Aguilera, 1998). In international mediation, numerous examples abound. At the wake of the eathquake in Haiti, the United Nations dispatched humanitarian assistance to the crisis-sticken island in order to quell further crisis occasioned by the earthquake. New Orleans received similar attention after hurricane Katrina. When Fukushima nuclear plant erupted due to the effects of tsunami, and displaced the people living in the area, the government of Japan activated some crisis intervention measures to cushion its devastating effect.

Conflict management involves implementing strategies to limit the negative aspects of conflict and to increase the positive aspects of conflict at a level equal to or higher than where the conflict is taking place (Rahim, 2002). In the days leading up to the outbreak of civil war between Nigeria and Biafra, the Quakers employed international mediation, to avoid an escalation in an already volatile situation. (Bercovitch, 2003).

One more failed measure involving international mediation was the meeting between Gowan and Ojukwu – the two gladiators in the war, in the so-called Aburi conference, which fell apart when both parties returned home. The governments of Gabon, Ireland, and the Vatican came to the aid of the losing Biafran side as part of the conflict management strategy.

Conflict Prevention: This refers to a variety of activities aimed at anticipating and averting the outbreak of conflict (Lund, 2002). Diplomacy is one major tool in international mediation, which, if properly applied could save a whole lot of problems. Successive American presidents have engaged in international mediation with leaders of Israel and Palestine in an effort to amicably settle their political differences. Although these efforts have not quelled conflicts in the region, they have demonstrated willingness of the leaders to bring about peace and harmony in the world.

Conflict Transformation is the process by which conflicts are transformed into peaceful outcomes. It recognises that contemporary conflicts require more than the reframing of positions and the identification of win-win outcomes (Miall, 2004) The referendum, which gave rise to the "Good Friday Agreement" in Northern Ireland was a result of a series of mediations involving almost every major country in Europe and beyond. Also in Arusha Tanzania on 4 August 1993, the government of Rwanda and the rebel Rwandan Patriotic Front (RPF) reached a negotiated agreement that ended a three-year Rwandan Civil War.

The tabulation below further explicates the terms for better understanding.

Conflict Management	Crisis Intervention	Conflict Prevention	Conflict Transformation
Power-sharing (E.g. Zimbabwe, where Robert Mugabe (ZANU Party) and Morgan Tsvangirai (MDC) share power. And in Kenya where Mwai Kibaki (PNU) and Raila Odinga (ODM) share political leadership).	Relief supplies (Eg. National Emergency Management Agency (NEMA and the United States government came to the aid of dwellers of New Orleans after horricane Katrina).	Peace-keeping mission. (Eg. Indian soldiers were mobilized to intervene in Somalia to avoid further breakdown of law and order.).	Restorative justice/ public hearings (Eg.Truth and Reconciliation Commission in South Africa after the apartheid regime).
_____	_____	Regional Organizations' mediation (Eg. Due to the election violence, the African Union sent delegation to Ivory Coast to find a way to mediate in the conflict).	Granting of Amnesty. (Eg. Amnesty granted by President Benigno Aquino III on alleged mutineers in the Philippines).
Use of Force (E.g. NATO air strikes against Bosnian Serbs influenced the Dayton Accords). (Sisk, 1996: 94).	Medical and food emergencies (Eg. The United Nations quickly sent much needed relief materials to Haiti after the massive earthquake, which destroyed the greater part of the country.)		_____
_____	_____		Referendum/ plebiscite. (Eg. "Good Friday Agreement" of Northern Ireland).
Economic Inducement (E.g. United States to Soviet Union).	Availability of world aid (E.g. Indonesia after tsunami).	Diplomatic summit (Eg. President Clinton's meeting with Israeli and Palestinian leaders at Camp Davis)	

II

MEDIATION

Not an actual mediation scene, by Dr. Davidson and Mrs. Stock, both staff of the John Carroll School, Bel Air, Maryland.

George and Jane were married for the past ten years and had no offspring. They blamed each other for the barrenness. It came to a point that they refused to talk to each other. Their friends and relatives offered to mediate in their feud, and were refused. So they lived in the same room not speaking to each other.

One morning, George had an appointment for a job interview. Since he had not had a job for months, he believed that was the main reason for the fight in the house. He therefore thought that the new job would be that magic wand to settle their domestic problem. The only huddle was how to wake up early enough to keep the appointment. He had no alarm clock, and as a heavy sleeper, he needed someone to wake him up early to make it to the bus stop.

Since he and Jane were the only ones in the house and were not on talking terms, he had difficulty communicating his request to his wife. Later in the middle of the night, he decided to pull a fast one. He wrote a note on a piece of paper and placed it on Jane's side of the bed. The note read: "please wake me up at five o'clock." When Jane woke up and saw the note, she replied on the flip side of the same note: "please, it is five o'clock, wake up", and placed it on the sleepy George. Of course, George did not see the note until he woke at about seven o'clock.

At that moment, George needed no diviner to tell him that his prospect for a job had become a tall dream. It was indeed the anticlimax of a ten-year old marriage. George and Jane gave room to an acrimonious relationship, which caused him a job as well as their marriage. Only if humility had prevailed, they would have welcomed mediators when the problem started brewing.

It is interesting to note that mediation has been in existence from the first day people started having misunderstanding.

It originally started in association with the court system, meaning that one had to be in the legal profession to mediate. "Today, however, interest in mediation is slowly developing in the cognate fields of psychology, sociology, social work, pastoral counseling and pastoral psychology" (Chan, 2007).

Mediation is the intervention of a neutral third party, who intervening at the request of the parties assists the parties at dispute in finding their own way out of the dispute through equity through consensus. It is any process for resolving disputes in which another person helps the parties negotiate a settlement (Chan, Leviton and Greenstone, Beer with Stief).

In his summation, Chan infers that "mediation is a process which involves three parties – a neutral third party and the two disputants who work towards the goal of reaching an agreement or a consensus" (2007). He, therefore, propounds 'assumptions' including, but not limited to, the following:

- Mediation assumes that people can resolve conflicts and are capable of discovering their own resources for doing so.
- Mediators define and control the structure of the process but seldom make suggestions or give advice.
- Disputants control the content of conflict issues and make the decision.
- Values, beliefs and attitudes are not the focus of mediation but can be discussed and may be useful in clarifying issues for both parties.
- Participants in a mediation are likely to carry out agreements because they are personally involved in making the decision and have a stake in the outcome.

In addition, it is noteworthy that "mediation assumes that the disputants have a desire and are willing to work within the process toward an amicable and mutual agreement or resolution" (Chan, 2007).

In the same vein, there are circumstances when it would be imprudent to pursue mediation. Citing Beer and Stief, Chan enumerated those circumstances including, but not limited to, the following:

- A serious incident has just occurred and people are still too upset to carry on a useful conversation.
- One party seems incapable of listening to anything you say, or seems otherwise too disturbed to negotiate a workable agreement.
- You believe that one party might be better off using the courts or other forum. Power imbalance makes fair agreement unlikely.
- Key parties are unwilling to participate. (2007).

Mediation is a serious business as well as a sensitive one. Therefore, if the setting is wrongly chosen and or arranged, the outcome might be regrettable. In the light of this, certain experts in mediation have adduced various aspects to consider in arranging for mediation. Some of the popular opinions include the fact that,

> The physical setting can have an impact on facilitating communication, gaining control of the argument, reducing or increasing pressure on the parties, and insuring the safety of all those involved. (Chan, Leviton, Greenstone).

Mediation experts emphasize the need to select a neutral venue for mediation. The reasoning here is "that the disputants must feel equally empowered" (2007).

Regarding the choice of site, some factors must be put into consideration, such as:

i. privacy
ii. sufficient lighting
iii. absence of distraction
iv. adequate space/ventilation
v. adequate security
vi. easy accessibility (2007).

General Rules For Mediation Setting

1. Everyone should be able to see and hear everyone else and participate easily in discussions.
2. Members of one party should be able to sit together if they choose. Couples typically want to sit side by side.
3. Everyone should be physically comfortable, undistracted, and feel as safe as possible.
4. The mediators should be able to control the process.
5. The setting should suggest mediator impartiality.
6. Pick a location that feels comfortable and private: not too large, not too dim or cluttered (Chan, Beer with Steief).

The suitable furniture for mediation is a round table or a square table, or a rectangular table. The sitting arrangement is strictly important.

Appropriate mediators should possess intelligence, tact, drafting skills, a sense of humor, and have specific knowledge and expertise of the conflict at hand. Mediators who possess these attributes are likely to be acceptable to all sides in a conflict, and consequently enhance the parties' motivation to reach a peaceful settlement. (Bercovitch).

Corroborating Bercovitch, Chan notes: the mediator is expected to be a neutral third party (2007). He further identifies some personality traits and skills of a good mediator:

- Strong people skills, especially giving good attention.
- Able to be directive and to confront.
- Comfortable with high emotions, arguments, interruptions, tears.
- Respected and trusted.
- Imaginative in solving problems.
- Patient as disputants inch their way towards resolution.
- Able to empathize and be gentle, to withhold judgment.
- Impartial: putting aside one's own opinions, reactions, and even some principles.
- Low need for recognition, credit, having things turn out your way (2007).

The talent is reflected in the sensitivity with which the mediator listens, hears, responds, empathizes, creates, draws parties into the process and deftly maneuvers through the delicate and difficult moments with an intuitive sense of timing and appropriateness (Chan, Leviton, Greenstone, Beer with Stief).

Many prominent scholars of mediation are of one accord regarding the place of mediation in human society. Chan, Bercovitck, Beer with Steif, Leviton, and Greenstone agree that the mediation process is a serious business, which requires the commitment of seasoned mediators possessing those qualities as enumerated above.

Mediation Process

The mediation process consists of four different stages, namely: i) Opening Statement, ii) Information Sharing and Issue Identification, iii) Exchange and Negotiation, iv) Agreement and Conclusion.

These four stages are discussed in details below:

Stage 1 -- Opening Statement.

The first thing in a mediation session is for the mediator and co-mediator to be aware of their role and place in the entire process. The mediator discusses the process, and describes the mediator's role, the roles of the participants, and the general expectations for the mediation (Chan, Myers, Filner).

Chan, Leviton and Greenstone, give the purposes of the Opening Statement as summarized below:

- establish a safe environment to negotiate
- establish the mediator's credibility and control of the proceedings
- explain the mediation process and what will be asked of the parties

- obtain necessary commitments from the parties concerning their involvement
- be sensitive to concerns raised by the parties (2007).

Before the actual commencement of mediation, the mediator must assure the disputants of his/her neutrality. The disputants must make a commitment to respect each other's time and values. "Expectations are also pointed out to the parties in regard to their commitment to the time required for resolving the issues, after which they are requested to provide their consent to commence the process." (2007).

Stage 2 - Information Sharing and Issue Identification

This stage involves data gathering. Chan, Leviton and Greenstone provide a concrete approach, thus:

1. Ask each disputant to state his/her perception of the conflict. Hear all evidence pertinent to the dispute. Collect any evidence relating to the dispute, such as written contracts, cancelled checks, receipts, and reports.
2. Clarify issues.
3. Clarify remaining differences and see whether the disputants can form a common understanding.
4. Listen actively to the disputants' issues and feelings as they are talking (2007).

Still in this stage, Chan mentions Leviton and Greenstone as proposing 'guidelines for the mediator in respect to the information that is provided as follows:'

1. Learn about the parties' interests and priorities.

2. Determine whether the parties agree on the credibility of the incidents and information.
3. Clarify the differences and see whether the parties can form a common understanding.
4. Formulate clear goals.
5. Attempt to settle simple issues. Build on success.
6. Note parties' underlying needs and hopes. These are at the core of the dispute. Having them addressed and met will be the core of a resolution (2007).

Stage 3 - Exchange and Negotiation.

"During this stage", according to Chan, "the disputants must take an active role and directly communicate their needs and interests". He also cites Leviton and Greenstone as inferring that "this will create the psychological ownership that will make the final agreement work" (2007).

It is understood that the third stage encompasses problem solving, but not limited to it. Beer with Stief is quoted as concluding that "The Building the Agreement phase is the time for parties to:

1. Identify and evaluate a range of ideas
2. Negotiate with everyone's interests in mind
3. Develop and test specific proposals
4. Gain confidence in their ability to resolve the situation and to build commitment to the emerging agreement. (2007).

Stage 4 – Agreement and Conclusion

An agreement between disputants "will contain all the statements that they have arrived at through a meeting of the minds." (2007).

Chan writes that Beer and Stief identify elements that an agreement should contain, namely;

1. Details specifics: who, what, when.
2. Is evenhanded and not conditional
3. Uses clear, familiar wording
4. Emphasizes positive action
5. Deals with any pending proceedings
6. Provides for the future (2007).

Mediator Styles

The four mediator styles are as listed below, namely:

i. Facilitative Mediation
ii. Transformative Mediation
iii. Evaluative Mediation
iv. Restorative Justice Mediation

The first three were the original styles of mediation. Later, Restorative Justice became part of the group.

Restorative Justice Mediation

Although last in the group, restorative justice is "a systematic response to wrongdoing that emphasizes healing the wounds of victims, offenders and communities caused or revealed by the criminal behavior" (*Mediation and Conflict Resolution Office*, 1999).

The main point in Restorative Justice Mediation is "identifying and taking steps to repair harm" (Chan). Another focal point here is to identify the nature and extent of the victim's loss and to explore how the offender might begin to repair the harm caused by the criminal act. Yet another important aspect is that "agreements are made concerning restitution schedules, follow-up meetings and monitoring procedures." (Chan, Van Ness & Strong).

Facilitative Mediation

Facilitative Mediation is the foremost style of mediation. In facilitative mediation, "the mediator structures a process to assist the parties in reaching a mutually agreeable resolution". One advantage of this style is that it empowers parties, and help the parties take responsibility for their own disputes and the resolution of the disputes. The flip side of this style is that mediation takes too long, and too often ends without agreement. (Zumeta, Chan).

Transformative Mediation

Transformative Mediation has certain distinctive features as succinctly discussed:

Transformative mediators leave responsibility for the outcomes with the parties.

Transformative mediators feel, and express a sense of success when empowerment and recognition occur, even in small degrees. They do not see a lack of settlement as a failure.

Transformative mediation has similar advantages and disadvantages as facilitative mediation. In addition, proponents of transformative mediation worry that outcomes can be contrary to standards of fairness and that mediators in these approaches cannot protect the weaker party. (Zumeta, Chan, Spangler, Baruch Bush, and Folger).

Evaluative Mediation

In evaluative mediation, the mediator structures the process, and directly influences the outcome of mediation. The kernel of this approach, therefore, is summarized in these words:

> In evaluative mediation, the mediator controls the process and suggests solutions for resolving the conflict. The focus of an evaluative mediation is primarily upon settlement. The mediators will make their best efforts to get the parties to compromise, if necessary, to achieve a result (Mediation and Conflict Resolution Office).

Of the four mediation styles, Facilitative Mediation seems to stand out. Reason for its prominence is that the mediator structures a process to assist the parties in reaching a mutually agreeable resolution (Zumeta). One advantage of this style is that it "empowers parties, and help the parties take responsibility for their own disputes and the resolution of the disputes. The flip side of this style is that mediation takes too long, and too often ends without agreement.

III
FACTORS INFLUENCING MEDIATION

Mediation And Culture

The Arab Spring breeze blew through the several regions of the world, encompassing several peoples and cultures. Therefore, any meaningful discussion on mediation must take into account the various cultural sensibilities of the regions of the world. To mediate on issues spanning the various regions of the world, therefore, the professional mediator must be culturally diverse. This section of the book defines culture and its relationship with mediation.

Culture is a representation of the customary beliefs, social forms, and material traits of a racial, religious, or social group; *also*: the characteristic features of everyday existence (as diversions or a way of life) shared by people in a place or time..." (*The Free Merriam-Weber Dictionary*).

An English Anthropologist defines culture as "that complex whole which includes knowledge, belief, art, law, morals, custom, and any other capabilities and habits acquired by man as a member of society" (Tylor).

Culture refers to the following Ways of Life, including but not limited to:

   i. ***Language***: the oldest human institution and the most sophisticated medium of expression.
  ii. ***Arts & Sciences***: the most advanced and refined forms of human expression.
 iii. ***Thought***: the ways in which people perceive, interpret, and understand the world around them.
  iv. ***Spirituality***: the value system transmitted through generations for the inner well-being of human beings, expressed through language and actions.
   v. ***Social activity***: the shared pursuits within a cultural community, demonstrated in a variety of festivities and life-celebrating events.
  vi. ***Interaction***: the social aspects of human contact, including the give-and-take of socialization, negotiation, protocol, and conventions (Roshan Cultural Heritage Institute).

It is often the case that cultural differences constitute the most common cause of misunderstanding between parties in dispute as well as between disputants and the mediator. In international mediation, some of the cultural differences might be religious, language, demeanor, et cetera. The challenging question then is how a mediator remains neutral and objective in the event that his/her cultural identity and philosophy differ from those of the disputants.

Familiarity with the culture of disputants is one way a mediator wins the trust of the disputants. For a mediator who finds self mediating in a different culture, the first approach would be to get to understand the people's culture by self education. Education in this regard is to ask questions from locals who are not directly connected to the dispute. The mediator should also spend time in the given environment, with a view to understanding how the people relate with people who do not belong to their cultural group. Reading about the people's cultural norms is yet another means of understanding the culture of any particular people.

Mediating in a culture different from one's culture could be cumbersome, but not impossible. In the event that a mediator is assigned to mediate in a dispute between people whose cultural norms differ from his/hers, the expected attitude would be that of empathy as opposed to a judgmental stance. If, for instance, a religion-neutral mediator gets an opportunity to mediate in a dispute between two religion-adherents, the prudent thing to do would be to probably start each session with a prayer led by one of the disputants in their own religious tradition. Should they not be keen in starting with a prayer, the session proceeds without the mediator's imposition of values, by letting them understand that it is all about them and their intention to settle their dispute, however they arrive at such settlement.

A mediator in a predominantly Muslim community must be sensitive and respect the fact that women cover, at least, their head in public. Therefore, a female mediator whose mission must succeed ought to identify with this dress code without losing her identity. If the disputants have diverse religions, it would be prudent to endeavor to avoid any religious trappings and direct all resources to the subject matter. This same understanding also goes for a male mediator. If his appearance would make him acceptable to the people, it would not be out of place to adorn flowing gowns and wear a goatee like the rest of them, without deviating from his mission.

Muslims tend to profoundly protect their females from exposure to external influences. Some even restrict women's place in society to consultative roles – mainly in domestic affairs. Some strict Muslims believe that women should neither be seen nor heard. To this effect, therefore, mediating in conflict in such culture may be prodigious. The United States State Department often sends emissaries and diplomats to the Islamic world. As commendable as this project is, it would be worth an effort to observe the emotional response of such cultures, and note that some Muslim communities perceive as insensitive, on the part of the United States, when female emissaries are sent to meet with their rulers who probably double as spiritual leaders, hence there may not be a marked separation of state and religion as in some Western cultures.

In terms of the emissaries and diplomats to the region, they should identify with the culture of the people and dress appropriately. If the Secretary of States were to meet with the Emir of Baghdad (as an example), though she is American and represents American interest, dressing like an average Iraqi woman for just that purpose would not make her less of a Secretary of State or less of an American.

Dressing like the people is a way of identifying with them. By identifying with them, there is less tension and suspicion by the people. This is where relationships begin to heal, and the people begin to develop trust in the American mission in the region.

Finally, a mediator – male or female must make concerted effort to resonate with the people's point of view as influenced by their environment. He/she must carefully and patiently listen to them in an effort to find a common ground toward the resolution of their dispute. This becomes important because cultural differences could be such a sensitive issue that might be misconstrued if not handled properly. In an international mediation, culture could make or mar a session.

For a mediator who finds himself/herself in a culture other than his/her cultural circle, it takes more than education to fit into the group. It takes tact, sensitivity, intelligence, tolerance and discipline to mediate in such environment. Such cross-cultural mediation is not as easy as it seems. It is only when the disputants trust the mediator and the mediator empathizes with the disputants that the hope of a successful mediation is possible.

When a mediator appreciates the importance of Cultural Empathy, mediation is half attained. Empathy, in this context, is defined as intellectual and emotional awareness and understanding of another person's thoughts, feelings, and behavior even that are distressing. It emphasizes understanding. When a mediator empathizes with disputants, the mediator creates a safe and balanced environment in which people can be heard as they wish to be heard. (*faculty.mc3.edu, Empatia Resolutions*).

Mediation And Language

Language is often the first barrier and at very least an ongoing challenge to any inter-cultural mediation. The problem of language is more intense when the disputants and the mediator come from different language groups, as in the case of many international mediation efforts, including mediating in the Arab world. Granted, the problem of language could be addressed by the use of an interpreter or translator, which is not without its own tension.

Language is a vital element in mediation. As a vital element, it has to be spoken and understood for it to achieve its intended outcome. If, for instance, a mediator intends to make inroads into and successfully mediate in a conflict between Israel and Palestine, a couple of things would be expected. If the mediator neither understands nor speaks Hebrew or Arabic, there has to be a common front in the form of forging an alliance with both sides by researching some common words and phrases in the languages. Again, if the Israeli and the Palestinian participants do not understand each other's language nor do they speak nor understand the mediator's language, it would be prudent to employ the services of a couple of interpreters or translators.

In order to engage the right interpreter or translator, the mediator must make sure that the interpreter or translator understands the whole purpose of mediation. The mediator must make sure that the interpreter/translator is transparent and neutral and is not in anyway sympathetic to either of the disputant's cause. For instance, questions regarding interpreter's opinion about the Jewish occupation of Gaza and West Bank could be a quick test of neutrality. Another question could be about his/her take on the independence of Palestine as a sovereign state. A denial or affirmation of the occupation, or a biased opinion over the Palestinian sovereignty would indicate subjectivity and a possible prejudgment.

To buttress this stance, the mediator could also remind him/her that the job of the interpreter is limited to being a liaison between the mediator and the disputants, and that his/her personal opinion is not part of the assignment.

Disputants, though eager to resolve their conflict, are also interested in a mediator with the following qualities: credibility, integrity, intelligence, knowledge of, and familiarity with the process – subject matter expert (SME).

In light of this situation, a mediator is expected to possess the following credentials:

- Assurance that he/she is seasoned in his/her profession.
- Reference to previous accomplishments and mediation successes.
- Verifiable educational background.
- Emphasis on his/her neutrality and transparency.
- His/her willingness to learn some rudiments of the disputants' language/s.
- Assurance of his/her familiarity with the history and culture of the Middle East (for instance) and the attendant religious, cultural and territorial disputes dating back to the ancient days.
- A reassurance that he/she has come with an approach aimed at brokering a lasting peaceful coexistence and tranquility to a people who have seem all sorts of disruption to normal living.

- An exhibition of an unbiased and genuine interest in their cause.

Finally, it is paramount that an adroit mediator should be mindful of expert opinions, which stipulate some type of mantra for mediators thus:

> Appropriate mediators should possess intelligence, tact, drafting skills, a sense of humor, and have specific knowledge and expertise of the conflict at hand. Mediators who possess these attributes are likely to be acceptable to all sides in a conflict, and consequently enhance the parties' motivation to reach a peaceful settlement (Bercovitch, 2003).

In summary, language barrier could make or mar a mediation process, the same way the use of translators is vital to the success or failure of a mediation setting.

Mediation and Power Balance

In mediation, *Power* is the careful consideration of who is being perceived as important or *powerful* in the mediation at any given time. Keeping the *power balanced* in mediation refers to the efforts made by the mediation through specific techniques to assure that each separate disputant is being equally heard and thereby given equal significance and equal respect and consideration for his or her perspective (Hope, 2010).

Power balance is so sensitive that it determines to a great extent the trajectory of any given session. Any perception of improper power balance is capable of derailing an otherwise successfully planned mediation. To put it in proper perspective, a detailed look at the various aspects will help to understand the concept of power balance.

- *Power balance between disputants*

Power balance enables disputants to present their issues on an equal basis. It facilitates an unbiased resolution of disputes by the parties involved in mediation. Notable scholars are of the opinion that the smaller the power difference between the two parties, the more successful will be the mediator (Bercovitch, Young).

- *Why power balance?*

Power balance is important because when disputants negotiate as equals, there is the plausibility of a successful resolution of dispute. It is also the case that "When disputants feel equally respected and that each have an equally important perspective they are free to let go of anger and their singular position. It frees them to consider the other side's perspective and consider how the other side may have valid and important perspectives also". Hope (2010). Again, where there is a power balance, none of the disputing parties will feel left out of the reconciliation process.

Where there is a power balance, the outcome of negotiation is often acceptable by the parties. Such agreements as reached in a power-balanced negotiation results from a relaxed atmosphere conducive for free expression and presentation of various sides to the case. As a result, individuals stand a better chance of accepting such agreements as binding and possibly lasting.

- Mediator's power balance between disputants

A good mediator usually allots equal and same amount of time to all disputants to express their concern and their own side of the story. He/she maintains a safe environment for both parties. He/she maintains a good amount of noticeable measure of neutrality in the course of mediation. When parties are able to relate on equal bases, they are more than likely to easily reach a quick and amicable resolution. This could only be attainable with a proper coordination of sequence of events in a mediation session.

- *Power balance crucial to insuring a lasting positive change*

When disputants negotiate as equals, they freely express their frustration. This freedom of expression gives rise to an amicable, unrestrained and possible lasting resolution of the conflict.

Where a mediator notices an apparent power imbalance between disputants, he/she must tactically ensure a balance without compromising neutrality. It is worthy of note that the mediator's obligation with regard to negotiation power is to ensure that each party in mediation has sufficient capacity to effectively represent their interests in mediation (*Oregon Mediation Center, Inc.*).

- Disputants' perception of mediator's status of power versus theirs

The perception of the disputants of the mediator's status of power is highly important. Some mediators are better able to marshal resources and be more persuasive. They possess leverage and can use social influence that could be crucial in persuading the parties to make concessions or move toward an agreement. In like manner, if the disputants do not respect the mediator as *valid* or a powerful enough figure, it might adversely affect their participation in mediation (Bercovitch, Hope).

Perception of power is as important as possession of actual power in mediation. Nonetheless, perception is never the same as reality. Perception is what a person makes of reality -

> If you conclude (perceive) that you are more powerful, you may relax and not prepare as well as you should. On the other hand, if you conclude (perceive) that you are weaker than the other side, there is a risk that you will be discouraged and again not devote sufficient attention to how you might persuade them (Ury, et al).

Perception of power, therefore, could be described as a double-edged sword, which if handled properly, could be a veritable tool; otherwise could cause irreparable harm either way.

- Perception of equal ground and power with disputants and mediator

Part of the skilled mediator's job is to assist the disputants to understand that both mediator and disputants are out for a common goal. It is taken for granted that both parties are on equal grounds and powers. Since it is an established fact that a successful mediation depends on the disputants' level of trust and confidence in the mediator and the entire process, it is up to the mediator to display how much familiar he is with their dispute. The onus is on the mediator to explain to the disputants that he/she is only a neutral mediator, with no vested interest in either party. The mediator must let the disputants understand that mediation depends on their willingness to resolve their dispute, realizing that the mediator is only an instrument (facilitator) to the process.

In order to keep the perception of equal powers present, the mediator may find the following steps so helpful:

I. Let the disputants understand that there is power in developing a good working relationship between each other.
II. Suggest that they seek power in understanding their interests.
III. Call their attention to the fact that to invent an elegant option is one important asset in mediation.
IV. Since using external standards of legitimacy is one source of power in mediation, disputants should, therefore, be helped to explore it.
V. Inform them that developing a good BATNA (Better Alternative To A Negotiated Agreement) is an important ingredient of empowerment in negotiation. More about BATNA later.

Can mediation of a conflict make the situation worse?

"Mediation can always make a conflict worse, and mediation often makes conflicts worse" (Hope). If the disputants notice even the slightest form of bias and prejudice by the mediator, anger might flare and the situation becomes worse than it was found. If the mediator exhibits ignorance and lack of proper knowledge of the bone of contention, he/she loses the ability to keep the situation under control. A mediator's arrogance and lack of respect for the people's cultural sensitivity could constitute grounds for an escalation of conflict. Sometimes, the disputants themselves are just not ready for the emotions that mediations bring up; and the mere fact that each shows up and see one another in mediation will make the conflict worse – because they say and do things there that may worsen the conflict (Hope).

Several examples exist in which a power imbalance led to a worsening of the conflict. The Argentine-British dispute over the Falkland Islands is a typical example of power imbalance leading to worsening of conflict. Alexander Haig (United States Secretary of State under President Ronald Reagan) who was mediating on behalf of the United States in the dispute proffered conditions, which turned out to be a clear case of power imbalance. Haig's effort to impose a solution heavily biased towards one of the disputants, forced Argentina into an underdog position it was unwilling to accept (Bercovitch). Of course, the resultant effect was that the British-Argentine struggle over the Falkland Islands snowballed into a crisis of international magnitude.

The lingering conflict between Israel and Palestine almost came to a crescendo when the United States recognized

Jerusalem as the capital of Israel. To add insult to injury, as it were, the United States later legalized the occupation of West bank, contrary to the status quo, which hitherto gave the territory its named "occupied territory". In these preceding examples, if the idea of such intervention was to make peace through territorial demarcation, the resultant effect was creation of more conflict.

How political leaders who are NOT involved in the mediation affect the mediation

Political leaders possess certain leverage, combined with *carrot and stick*, which they wield through their representatives. Government sponsored mediators are often influenced by political leaders, who sometimes have ulterior motives. Again, rich political leaders make bogus financial promises to entice less-privileged disputants to settle for less. Often the difficulty encountered by a mediator lies not with the negotiators but with their constituents, up the communication chain, who seem unsupportive of the terms or are unwilling to make the concessions deemed necessary by the mediator (Bercovitch).

It is imperative to note that the two political leaders must be supportive of mediation because if either is not supportive – then the mediation will be in danger of being compromised and the conflict could easily worsen to a crisis stage (Hope). This seems to be the case with each successive mediation move between Afghan Tliban and United States leaders. Crises resume where mediation fails.

- If something goes wrong in a mediation

If, in the course of mediation, the parties become intolerant of each other, a tactical mediator would arrange to meet with each party separately—this is often considered the last resort. If one party feels that the other is getting more attention, the mediator ought to reiterate the principle of neutrality, which means fairness to both sides. If the problem is environmental, the mediator should consider a shift of venue. A neutral and pleasing location should be carefully selected to begin with, to avoid simple environmental conflicts (Hope). This does not just play out in mediation. In sports, there is what is called the home advantage, in which case the visiting team often assumes an imbalance and somewhat hostile stance by supporters of the home team. The supporters might just be cheering as patriots who love their team. The visiting team might misconstrue this otherwise innocent cheering as denigration. In many cases, this assumption usually wins the game for the home team even though they may not be better than the visiting team. So, neutrality and fairness are two most important elements for a balanced mediation.

- Signs of successful mediation

One indicator that mediation is going well is when disputants are able to present their concerns in a less-acrimonious manner. Another good sign is when they are willing to listen to one another, with a view to reach a balanced settlement. Yet another sign is when they develop a cordial and mutual relationship with the mediator. This is an outcome that every mediation session wishes for. Nonetheless, it is a far cry for many mediation sessions.

– Contingency plan in conflict escalation

When disputants express frustration and discontentment at the direction of a mediation process, it is a clear sign that a conflict is escalating. At this juncture, a good mediator needs to re-strategize and effectively change the course of mediation. The failure of disputants to continue with any form of mediation is indicative of an escalation of conflict. A good course of action at this juncture is to reach out to the chief antagonists in the conflict. There is no guarantee that this approach will result to an agreement. However, there is high probability of success with an experienced mediator wielding a strategized approach.

IV

MEDIATION TECHNIQUES

Mediation is a systematic discipline, with its own language and procedure. It is only when these forms are observed that a meaningful and successful mediation is achievable. In this regard, therefore, it is extremely important that anyone aspiring to successfully mediate in conflicts must be acquainted with these techniques. It is moreover necessary in multi-cultural settings.

- Going To The Balcony

William Ury states that "balcony" is a metaphor for a mental attitude of detachment. Going to the balcony means distancing yourself from your natural impulses and emotions. From the balcony you can calmly evaluate the conflict, almost as if you were a third party. You can think constructively for both sides and look for a mutually satisfactory way to resolve the problem. (1991, 17).

When a five-year old throws a tantrum, he gets *a timeout*; when the five-year-old spirit inside a full-grown man manifests in an argument, he *goes to the balcony*. Going to the balcony in this context means taking a break to reflect on the preceding event. Such temporary retreat is a time to evaluate the situation before making a commitment or taking a major decision.

Eddy and his father got into an argument regarding when to return home at night. Eddy's father had repeatedly warned him over the danger of coming home past 6.00 PM. Eddy always gives the excuse that he works late. At sixteen years he is not expected to be working that late, says his father. Since his family is not capable of supporting him financially, he works to take care of some minor bills. His father understands all this fact, but is still concerned about his safety in a rough neighborhood.

One evening, Eddy came home with a black eye. This was the opportunity his father was waiting for. His father cashed in on this opportunity to hold a meeting. The meeting was so heated that father and son stopped short at getting physical. Eddy vowed not to give up his job. Father offers a stern warning that Eddy must leave the house. Eddy had just started packing his few belongings when his father walked out of the room.

His father stayed in the bedroom for about ten minutes. When he remerged, Eddy was expecting another round of yelling and marching orders. Instead, father stretched out both his arms, invited Eddy to a warm embrace. At first, Eddy was reluctant to respond because he did not know what suddenly became of his father. With hands outstretched still, his father walked up to Eddy who was busily packing up to leave, held him as both embraced each other and shed tears like little babies.

Eddy's father muttered: I am only worried that you might be hurt; I did not mean to be hard on you. Eddy promised to discuss a change of work schedule with his supervisor.

What transpired in the above example is a case of "going to the balcony" to find a solution to an argument. Eddy stuck to his position of keeping his job. His father maintained his interest in the safety of his son. Since both were reluctant to budge, his father finally took a time out, stepped aside for ten minutes. This was an opportunity for father and son to douse their tension and come to an agreement.

Going to the balcony is in no way punitive. If anything, it is highly recommended that people take a break, 'spread their wings', count to ten, inhale and exhale deeply to clear their brain and mind before making a clear, conscious, non-coerced, free commitment.

- Step To Their Side & Reframe

There is a wise saying that when a conscienceless power meets a powerless conscience, the former laughs first, and the latter laughs last. Of course, it is a known fact that he who laughs last laughs best. The Scriptures have it that if your adversary demands that you walk one mile, prepare to walk two miles (*paraphrased*).

In negotiation, affirming your opponent's stance is one tool to disarm him / her. Playing the fool, while focusing on the end product, is an important tactic to win over an opponent.

Stepping to their side, therefore, means playing along with a fellow disputant, with an aim to douse his/her anger and frustration. The end result of which is an amicable agreement. It is likened to a psychological redirection. The difference is that in redirection, the plan is to get the person exhibiting the behavior to focus on something else, different from the potential dangerous behavior.

In the same vein, *reframe* is a negotiation technique whereby one disputant changes the other from positional bargaining to problem-solving negotiation. "Reframing means taking whatever your opponent says and directing it against the problem". (Ury 1991).

One rainy night, a rapist broke into a family home and ordered the female occupant to lie on the floor. The courageous woman first pretended to take off he top and suddenly turned to the rapist and suggested that they do it quietly in the inner room. At that point the rapist cringed, stopped yelling orders and instead of going to the room, quietly beat a retreat towards the front door.

He was disarmed because contrary to his expectation of resistance, she softened up. He did not know what the woman was up against. Many such examples exist where a right approach leads to diffusion of an otherwise tense situation.

A certain pastoral worker in Lagos Nigeria recounted how he escaped an apparent carjacking or, at worst, armed robbery. He recalls returning from a communion round (visit to the sick) and was driving a church marked Peugeot car in the twilight of one Saturday evening on an ever-busy twenty-second road in FESTACT Town, Lagos. At the intersection of twenty-second and another busy street corner, a man called out "Father (But the pastoral worker was only a seminarian), can you give me a ride to the parish house, we have a prayer meeting". The pastoral worker did not recognize his face, nor did he pride himself of knowing everybody in a parish of more than five thousand families. He also suspected that this individual did not know him. If he did, he would not have called him "Father". He thinks that the man recognized the church car and not the driver. He, however, decided to give the man a ride. After they drove past the busy area the passenger orders the driver to stop. A quick instinct set in as the driver suspected that passenger was up to something. He did not stop him, nor did he argue with him. He simply suggested to the passenger not to waste his bullet or waste his energy. He further reminded him that he was willing to surrender the car keys quietly. At this point, the seeming petrified passenger remained speechless and only staring at the driver as the car rolled slowly to the next busy junction. As the car finally stopped he alighted; and before he got off, he looked straight in the driver's eyes and remarked: "You are lucky". The driver's apprehension heightened as he was confused about that remark.

Reminiscing on the whole drama, driver is able to reconstruct the scene thus: "Looking back now, I can understand that he did not become violent because he felt I was willing to cooperate. In reality, I was not willing to give up the car just like that. My plan was to speed off with him to the nearest police station, making sure he did not struggle the steering with me. Luckily, it all ended without further escalation due to my ability to remain calm and cooperative – *stepping to his side*.

- Building A Bridge

Building a golden bridge means making it easier for your opponent to surmount the four common obstacles to agreement: It means actively involving him in devising a solution so that it becomes his idea, not just yours; it means satisfying his unmet interests; it means helping him save face; and it means making the process of negotiation as easy as possible (Ury, 1991).

In some sense, the concept of *Building A Bridge* is equivalent to the idea of *giving people a rope to hang themselves*. 'Hanging' in this context is that the outcome of the decision is solely on the individual who accepts the suggestions and implements them. Resisting the urge to argue with the opponent is a strategy, which requires extra discipline, in order to achieve a common understanding. Not many decisions reached through this process are easily regrettable.

As part of the administration's immigration policy, the United States president, Trump, built fences and barriers on its southern borders. Some opponents of the policy cautioned that it was better to *build bridges* than barriers. Although the argument centers on physical bridge and barrier, it later pivots to psycho-socio building of bridge and barrier.

The psycho-socio aspect of the argument is that the southern neighboring countries were convinced to absorb certain categories of immigrants in exchange for some economic inducements. The final outcome of this bilateral immigration agreement is that both parties seem satisfied with the deal: the USA seems to have a break from surging immigrants; the

Mexican government seems economically empowered to share in the immigration policy.

- Power To Educate

Education plays a vital role in virtually every aspect of human transaction and at every level of human development and existence. In mediation, the *power to educate* is so important and has proven effective in reaching a workable agreement. As a mediation technique, *power to educate* enables one disputing party to let the other know the consequences of his/her inflexibility. It also allows the disputants to choose between options, which hitherto were not salient. The technique gives room for asking reality-testing questions: what do you think I will do? What will you do? These are the types of questions that elicit answers, and this is where the *power to educate* comes in.

Politicians anywhere in the universe wear the same or similar garbs. For the purpose of the subject matter, Washington, DC is a case study. It is no news that lawmakers try to outdo one another each time there is a fresh piece of legislation. In recent days, politicians have devised ways and means to hand-twist one another. One such example played out during the debate on extention of tax breaks and other matters. Democrats, on one hand, asked questions bordering on what happens to the one hundred and sixty million (160,000,000) middle class American workers who might see an average of twenty-dollar ($20.00) increase in their taxes if the break was not extended for two months. The Republican Party, on the other hand, argued that two months extension of such break was not just good for the tax-paying Americans.

At the end of the entire protracted debate, the Democrats used questions to *educate* the Republicans, using the argument of the hardships families would endure if their taxes went up in the New Year. Both parties also made compromises, thereby *building bridges* for each other to accede to a two-month extension of tax breaks for millions of Americans.

- Turning Adversaries into Partners

It is a natural reaction to meet force with force. When people are in conflict, the tendency is to out-maneuver the opponent, present a stronger argument and logic in order to curry people's sympathy and in turn win the case. But in a negotiated settlement, almost the opposite is the case. In mediation, moving against the current strengthens the resolve of the skilled mediator. This means that instead of engaging in a natural flow of countering the opponent's position, you do the unexpected thing of tactically concurring with the opponent, thereby going against his/her adversarial expectation. This tactic is capable of disarming a hardened opponent.

Eric and Jacy were married for over 20 years and were blessed with two children: a boy and a girl. At a point in their union, they had differences they could not resolve. Finally, they had to separate. After separation, they could not agree on a sharing formula of their estate, as well as custodial issues of their 16 and 14-year old children. They approached the court which referred them to mediation. Mediation was effective in the case of sharing the estate. However, one of the two children – the girl – has taken advantage of the family dysfunction to carve her own lifestyle, which was not in tandem with their family values.

Eric and Jacy exchange blames for their daughter's lifestyle. With the mediator's intervention, both come to the conclusion that hope is not lost for the rehabilitation of their wayward daughter. Both parents miraculously team up, bring their girl home, and finally decided that mother should take the greater part of the custody of their children, pending when they are old enough to choose their preferred residence. Due to this resolution, father further cedes part of his own portion of the estate to mother. All parties to dispute are happy, and the mediator feels some pride of fulfillment. Parents are able to bury the hatchet by momentarily forgetting their differences for the good of their common interest, in this case – daughter.

In summary, these techniques are not etched in stone, and there is no one-fits-all measure to it. However, a seasoned mediator would always find ways to work with these techniques in order to find amicable resolution of conflicts. The following scenarios are pointers to the fact that mediation can either be successful or deadlocked depending on approach.

In his book *Getting Past No*, William Ury notes,

Just as the best general never has to fight, so the police never had to use force. They used their power not to attack Van Dyke, but to contain him and educate him that his best alternative lay in surrendering peacefully. They brought him to his senses, not his knees. (1991).

This summary of a hostage encounter between the New York Police Department and a fugitive, Van Dyke, who escaped from the prison and took hostage of hospital employees, is a conglomeration of the entire five steps of breakthrough negotiation. The negotiator sounded like wonting to accede to the hostage-taker's demands, yet not losing track of his mission. A good negotiator never gives up nor does he/she easily cave in under pressure. He uses all his skills to save an otherwise hopeless situation and to save both life and save face.

The concept of face-saving "refers to maintaining a good self image" (*Conflict Research Consortium,* University of Colorado). Some examples will further clarify the concept.

Scenario One:

During the 2011 United States Republican Party presidential primaries, Herman Cain, a Republican presidential contender addressed the press and announced the suspension of his presidential campaign. For an ordinary American, Mr. Cain suspended his campaign, period. But between him and his accusers, he tactically beat a retreat to avoid further embarrassment by the barrage of accusations of impropriety by different women. Mr. Cain probably adhered to Ury's recommendation that negotiators "go slow to go fast." (1991). His moving slowly might have helped him trade minor concessions, and focus more on what he gained (face-saving) than on what he lost by withdrawing from the campaign.

Scenario Two:

In September of 2004, a militant group in Russia invaded a school in Beslan, North Ossetia, taking hostage of students, teachers, and guests. According to *CBS NEWS*, "The terrorists wanted Russian President Vladimir Putin to announce the withdrawal of all troops from Chechnya".

The Russian authorities responded by moving in troops and tanks. At the end of the three-day siege, involving more than 1,200 hostages, "officials say 330 died – 176 of them children. More than 500 others were wounded, and 24 children are now orphans. (*CBS NEWS*).

The Russian government was not new to crises of that magnitude, nor was there any doubt regarding its capability to handle terrorism-related hostages. However, Russia's approach to Beslan hostage standoff called to question its ability to effectively apply negotiation techniques.

Everything went wrong with the entire situation. The government moving troops and tanks challenged the hostage-takers' power. The hostage-takers did not have an escape route.

Since their demand was centered on the withdrawal of government troops from Chechnya, a skilled negotiator would *reframe* the militants' demand by tactically agreeing with them that the presence of the troops was inconveniencing. A skilled negotiator would *educate* them that the presence of troops in Chechnya was for the protection of the people's lives and property. The government should not have surrounded the school with tanks and armored personnel. Instead, a negotiator would have *built a bridge* by making a possible escape route for the hostage takers to exit the building when they got frustrated with the stalemate. At the end of the operation, the intention would not have been to *bring the militants to their knees, but to their senses*. This would have been achieved by letting them understand that the children have no place in government's decision to maintain troop's presence in Chechnya, nor is the school part of government bargaining chip.

Since the hostage situation went on for three days, the militants certainly were hungry or sleepy at one point or the other. A negotiator would have *stepped to the side* of the militants by making sure they had something to eat or drink. They might shun the offer, but the idea of offering might be that magic moment, which would have saved hundreds of lives, helped both militants and government save face. But the government's show of raw force directly and indirectly led to the death of innocent people who have no stake in the politics of the region.

V

PSYCHOLOGICAL LEGITIMACY OF MEDIATION

Logotherapy

Mediation is a concrete human endeavor, impacting human behavior. Therefore, any study of mediation must involve elements of psychology relevant to aspects under discussion. One such aspect is the importance of Logotherapy in conflict resolution.

Viktor Emil Frankl developed Logotherapy coined from Logos, a Greek word, which denotes meaning. He espouses logotherapy in the following statement: The freedom of will; the will to meaning; the meaning of life, these are the concepts upon which logotherapy is based (Frankl, 1988).

Scholars describe Frankl's lofty ideals at different fora, in different terms. He was an intellectually precocious child… even before finishing high school, he had begun a scientific correspondence with Sigmund Freud. He received his Doctor of Medicine degree in 1930 from the University of Vienna. He, thereafter, continued his training in neurology at the Psychiatric University Clinic (Graber, Chan).

One rather outstanding achievement of Dr. Frankl is his ability to galvanize hope for the seeming hopeless young people of the poverty-stricken era in his country. After the Great Depression, he began to set up counseling centers in Austrian cities in 1930, primarily for students and the unemployed. Viktor got enmeshed in the Nazi onslaught in 1942; almost his entire family perished in the hands of the Nazis. He survived the concentration camp because his camp was liberated in 1945 (Chan).

Logotherapy focuses on the meaning of human existence as well as on man's search for such meaning. Although logotherapy is placed in the same psychotherapeutic category as existentialism, Frankl further describes it in these words:

> In contrast to most of the existentialist schools of thought, logotherapy is in no way pessimistic, but it is realistic in that it faces the tragic triad of human existence: pain, death and guilt. Logotherapy may justly be called optimistic, because it shows the patient how to transform despair into triumph (1988).

From the foregoing, it could be appropriate to conclude that logotherapy is concrete and directly influences human behavior. It directly applies to mediation practices.

Three pillars of logotherapy are as follows:

- Life has meaning under all circumstances
- People have a will to meaning
- People have freedom under all circumstances to activate the will to meaning and to find meaning (Sjolie, Chan).

From the above stipulations, it could be inferred that there is no universal application to the 'rule'. Some individuals hold to the fact that they are born into a certain situation, and there is nothing they can do to change it. For persons in this category, the statement: *People have freedom under all circumstances to activate the will to meaning and to find meaning* does not necessarily apply. This is also the case with people often described as frustrated. These are people, who have practically reached the end of the street, and for them, life has no meaning, and there is no need struggling to change things around because it is not going to yield any meaningful result. For Frankl,...every individual is endowed with freedom, but because of the finiteness of the human being, there are some limitations to freedom in addition to other aspects of humanity...the freedom of man is a freedom within limits (Chan).

On the other hand, this pre-deterministic attitude has come under scrutiny as Frankle asserts that each person is ultimately self-determining. He believes that each individual has the freedom to change the direction of his or her life; and, consequently self-determine who one will become (2007).

Self-determination could be summed up as a combination of nature and nurture. This being the case, therefore, individuals can determine their trajectory and alter their destiny under certain circumstances – including the circumstances of birth. For instance, an individual who is born into a war-raved region could become a harbinger of peacekeeping. The same goes for someone who is born into abject poverty becoming a great philanthropist. All of these do not happen by sheer serendipity; they come at a great cost, involving self-disciple and sacrifice of pride and pleasure. Individuals who believe that somethings are part of their nature, which they can do nothing to change, give in to the idol of indolence that culminates in self-destruction.

The relevance of this to mediation is easily notable. Disputants often struggle to resolve their conflict. Even though they are determined to reach an agreement, they often fail due to a combination of factors. Such factors might include, but not limited to lack of assistance, occasioned by international bureaucracy, coupled with the fact that mediation involves other disputants who may not always agree to a resolution. In a situation like this, such effort gets frustrated and disputants return to *status quo ante*. The failure, therefore, is not entirely the disputants', but certain infiltrating elements contribute to obstruction of the achievement of mediation result.

Another poignant issue in Frankl's theory is the *Existential Vacuum*. It manifests itself mainly in a state of boredom – a sense of *meaninglessness and emptiness*; an inner void and apathy. If it persists in a person, it progresses into existential frustration. Individuals entrapped in this model try to fill the existential vacuum with drugs and violence. Other tools include food, over-work, sports, and entertainment. But the evil of it all is that such individuals remain unfulfilled in spite of these distractions (Chan).

This aspect is usually helpful in today's family mediation. Many a home has either broken or remained dysfunctional due to the *existential vacuum* of its members. Some attribute it to economic factors; others believe it is all about dissatisfaction in relationships. Irrespective of the reason/s, the end product is that individual members resort to some kind of escape route out of their frustration, including the use of drugs, violence and other social vices. Some even vent their frustration on the entire society, by resorting to armed robbery, rape, and other illicit activities.

Dr. Frankl seemingly implicates education when he writes, In an age of existential vacuum, we have said, education must not confine itself to, and content itself with, transmitting traditions and knowledge, but rather it must refine man's capacity to find those unique meanings, which are not affected by the crumbling of universal values. This human capacity to find meaning hidden in unique situations is conscience. Thus education must equip man with the means to find meanings. Instead, education often adds to the existential vacuum (1988).

Some educated people are highly depressed and find little meaning in life. Little wonder that such people metaphorically passed through education, but education did not pass through them. They gained a lot of theoretical experience of education with little to show for the practicality of education. Science and technology have contributed immensely to the advancement of the modern man. In the same token, the same science and technology have *conspiratorially* destroyed the mysteries surrounding human existence, thereby reducing man to merely a consumer of goods and services. Most of the things human beings produced, including services they provided, which gave them a sense of dignity, satisfaction and productivity, have been assigned to robots and computers. What then is left for the idle man? Humans then dissipate their reserved energy and time in suicide, homicide, terrorism, armed robbery, genocide because they are frustrated and find little meaning and reason for existence.

Peacekeeping and Existential Vacuum

Conflict is a universal phenomenon, with no marked boundaries. The Arab world seems to have noticed a fair share of conflicts and therefore serves as a focal point in this context. The region, with its influential cultural diversity, is capable of harnessing the rich potential of its teeming youth who sometimes resort to violence due to the effect of existential vacuum and somewhat unguarded indoctrination by religious and political leaders. It was the failure of the old brigade, vis-à-vis the political elite, to positively engage the people that partly gave rise to the Arab spring, which swept through the region and in the process swept away notable political despots.

With the simmering wave of conflicts all over the world, it would be futile to preach peace without finding the root cause of prevailing resentments. Numerous avenues abound in an effort to address issues bordering on conflicts. However, the willpower to confront these issues is what seems at bay with politicians and world leaders. One way of unifying the populace or at least enlightening the people is to reach out to schools to incorporate diversity awareness in their curricula. It is not just enough to start early to teach children the recital of the holy books. If their knowledge of the holy books were combined with their sense of unity, the Arab world would regain its glory as the region with rich cultural and educational base. This will, in turn, bring about lasting peace and security as well as prosperity in a region free of superstition. This is a challenge to the new Arab Spring leaders.

Peacekeeping and Psychotherapeutic Techniques in Logotherapy

Frankl (1988) developed the following topics: Socratic Dialogue; Paradoxical Intention; Dereflection. These topics will be briefly discussed in relation to the subject matter.

The Socratic Method (Socratic Dialogue) is a form of cooperative argumentative dialogue between individuals, based on asking and answering questions to stimulate critical thinking and to draw out ideas and underlying presuppositions (The Free Encyclopedia). It helps to bring the therapeutic process to the core issue of *where is the meaning in your life?* The whole aim is to make client independent of the therapist by helping him/her find his/her guidance within (2007).

Paradoxical Intention is the deliberate practice of a neurotic habit or thought, undertaken to identify and remove it. In Paradoxical Intention, the patient is encouraged to do, or wish to happen, the very things he fears engenders an inversion of intention. The pathogenic fear is replaced by a paradoxical wish (2007).

Dereflection strengthens our capacity for self-transcendence – our ability to reach out beyond self-centeredness toward other people or goals that are meaningful to us (2007). Community service and other charitable acts are some of the virtues that can *dereflect* a patient from hyper-reflection. At this instance, the patient's focus is redirected to positive activities beneficial to other members of society, including the elderly, the poor and helpless children. In the process, the patient gets some measure of healing, by focusing on reaching out to other people instead of focusing on his/her own problems, which could be overwhelming.

The relevance of all these to mediation is that for disputants to find meaning in life, they must struggle to go beyond those aspects that stand between their personal pride (positional bargaining) and the general interest of the community. It is at this level that mediation begins. Mediation is a personal decision, which starts from within the individual disputant's resolve to discuss the problem.

According to Frankl, Logotherapy's concept of man is based on three pillars:

- the freedom of will
- the will to meaning
- the meaning of life.

It should be noted that man's freedom is no freedom from conditions but rather freedom to take a stand on whatever conditions might confront him (1988).

It, therefore, behooves one to determine one's attitudes to pain and guilt – this is where freedom of choice comes into play. However, if one is fated for a situation, there is little one can do to alter it. Although fate cannot be changed, one may well change one's attitude to fate.

Logotherapy qualifies as a catalyst, not prescribing solution but directing the individual towards finding solution and meaning, based on life experiences and situations. It is concerned with the individual's existential aspiration and frustration (2007).

From the foregoing, it could be concluded that mediators are both pacemakers and peacemakers. Note that pacemakers "confront us with meanings and values...[peacemakers] alleviate the burden of meaning confrontation" (Chan). Either a *pacemaker* or *peacemaker* the mediator's role in the psychological wellbeing of disputants is inestimable.

In mediation, the mediator assists the disputants to move into the *noetic* dimension. According to Chan, this is where they are able to engage each other with intentionality and creativity in solving their problem, based on their ethical sensitivity, activation of conscience, understanding of values, and search for meaning (2007).

It could be asserted that mediation is synonymous with peacemaking, and that peacemakers must at all time and at all levels remain neutral and have a positive outlook toward the success of mediation. However, in some cases, this whole principle seems not to enjoy universal applicability.

Numerous examples exist to buttress this point. One such instance is when Saddam Hussein of Iraq allegedly annexed Kuwait, the United Nations intervened at the level of mediation. Mediation had hardly crumbled or come to a deadlock before the allied forces sent troops into Iraq, an action, which eventually culminated in the hanging of Saddam and others.

The logical opinion, from mediation point of view, is that both Saddam and the people of the region were not allowed to exercise their *ethical sensitivity, activation of conscience, understanding of values, and search for meaning* (2007). International mediators were not able to exhaust their strategies before the over-exuberant allied forces' bullets started ricocheting. Saddam would have been given a chance to explain his action. Shuttle diplomacy between Saddam and the Kuwaitis would have been activated to see how best to resolve their conflict. The action of the allied forces, therefore, denied mediators one major function of mediation, which is to help the parties in a dispute discover and articulate the wisdom which they brought to the mediation (2007).

From the example of Saddam Hussein, it could be understood that mediation, applying the Franklian principle, would handle the situation differently. A logotherapeutic mediator would assist the leader to discover for himself the meaning of his action, the outcome and implication in his leadership, in his personal life and in the lives of the citizens. At the end of it, they make an informed choice, which could be either wrong or right. But most often would lead to right choices because it also involves conscience formation. As Thomas Aquinas would admonish that people should follow their conscience because an informed conscience never goes wrong. The human capacity to find meaning hidden in unique situations is conscience (1988).

While mediation and logotherapy share certain commonalities, their aim and purpose tend to slightly differ. While the main goal in mediation is peace with an agreement between disputants, logotherapy or Franklian psychology is aimed at discovery of meaning through change of attitudes (2007). Their nexus is found in the peace of mind that comes with a negotiated settlement.

Logotherapy - a case-study

This author has engaged in a number of informal mediation of parent-child conflicts. The most recent was a case of a child who played truancy in school. Her parents believed that she went to school every day. Instead, the child would go loiter at a local shop and came back when she knew school was over. She was not lucky all the way. She soon fell prey to child predators. When eventually she was discovered, it was too late for her to claim innocence anymore. Her parents were angry with her on one side, she was angry with herself for her mistakes on the other hand. Parents asked her to leave their home.

With the intervention of a mediator through the instrumentality of a Catholic group, the child was helped to realize her folly as parents were made to understand the implications of sending her out of the house. The parties did not go all out to analyze what went wrong. Instead, mediator presented the realities of the situation, from the viewpoint of the mistakes made by the child as well as the resultant effect of sending her out in the dark. At the end of the meeting, both parents and child literally forgot the truancy case and focused on remedying the triggers of the child's behavior.

The main fact of logotherapeutic technique is to help the patient face the worst of his/her fears and anxiety. In colloquial terms, it is often said that things get worse before they get any better. A mother once told a story of how curious her son was, even as a toddler. She said her son liked the blue flame of the paraffin lantern. He would crawl up to the lamp stand, climb the chair and try to catch the flame. She was so alarmed that he would either fall from the chair or burn himself. No matter how she tried to keep him away from the lamp, he would cry and try the next minute to catch the flame. One day she watchfully allowed him to touch the flame. After touching the flame and was scalded, he cried and shrieked to the point of a mild fever. Call it child endangerment, but definitely not negligence. Rather, it could qualify as child empowerment. The effect of the experience is that it marked the beginning of the end of the child's attempt to try to catch the flame ever again.

The mother in this scenario was likely not a logotherapist, but she started using logotherapeutic techniques long before the publication of Dr. Frankl's book. It worked for her; hopefully, it would work for experts even more; only the correct application can make it happen.

Logotherapy endeavors to help people find meaning, fulfillment, contentment, and purpose in life. Logotherapy, is widely believed to be more pragmatic than some other psychological principles, especially as pertains to mediation. There is no doubt that all the psychological principles have their relevance in human existence. But in comparison with other psychological principles, Logotherapy is believed to be more outstanding, as George Orwell would assert: All animals are equal, but some are more equal.

Mediation is such a complex and diverse topic traversing several spectra of humanity. Therefore, the subheadings below address some of the relevant topics akin to the psychological and physiological aspects of mediation as treated in this work. The relevance is that a clear knowledge and understanding of a situation is the beginning of the solution. Any mediator's mastery and application of these terms will be that silver bullet to understand the nature of disputes and be prepared to meet disputants at their own comfortable levels. The behavioral pattern of the disputants may not always exhibit, but a mediator with a foreknowledge of human behaviors will certainly work successfully with anyone, irrespective of their attitude to mediation.

Crisis Intervention refers to the methods used to offer immediate, short-term help to individuals who experience an event that produces emotional, mental, physical, and behavioral distress or problems" (*Encyclopedia of Mental Disorders*). Example: At the wake of the eathquake in Haiti, the United Nations dispatched humanitarian assistance to the crisis-sticken island in order to quell further crisis occasioned by the eathquake.

Conflict Management is the long-term management of disputes and conflicts, which may or may not lead to resolution (*The President and Fellows of Harvard College, 2010*). Example: In the days leading to the outbreak of civil war between Nigeria and Biafra, the Quakers employed international mediation, to avoid an escalation in an already volatile situation (Bercovitch).

Conflict Prevention is reducing conflict that comes from behavior and ways of communicating that create unnecessary, unresolvable conflicts. It's about learning to say things in ways that do not get people's defenses up. It's a tool for the resolution of issue-based conflict, not a way of avoiding it (*Conflict*, 2010). Example: A truck bomb exploded at the World Trade Center in New York City on February 26 killing six people and injuring hundreds more. His (Clinton's) reaction was one of conflict avoidance—he said little about aggression of the enemy, nothing about blaming, and focused solely on hardship, mentioning the issue very briefly in his weekly radio broadcast (Feste).

Conflict Transformation usually denotes truth and reconciliation measures and commissions. Meetings form between factions of both sides that are able to peaceably talk to one another and efforts are made to promote understanding and empathy and stimulate healing of past harm done (Hope). Example: The referendum, which gave rise to the *Good Friday Agreement* in Northern Ireland was a result of a series of international mediations, involving almost every major country in Europe and beyond.

VI

TERRORISM

It is often believed that the promise for *seventy black-eyed virgins* in paradise is an irresistible allurement, which spurs men to take to suicide terrorism. But it takes only a greedy and less-intelligent young man to fall for that. To manage one black-eyed virgin is already a tedious job. To think of managing seventy of such species is insane. Again, thinking about it, if paradise were a peaceful and holy place, as we understand it, how would a holy and peace-loving God set up a chaotic and promiscuous situation just to reward the suicide bomber after destroying God's creation on earth?

In recent memory, the Arab world has been replete with all forms of conflict. This is not to conclude that violence is domiciled in that part of the world or to believe that the Middle East has a monopoly of violence. The menace of terrorism has become so widespread that insecurity has become the order of the day allover the human world. Did terrorists hijack any aspect of the Arab Spring? Could mediation have been employed in advance of any intended terrorist activity? These are rhethotical questions, which might not get answered even by the perpertrators of the Arab Spring protests.

A couple of definitions will go a long way in demystifying the secrecy enshrouding the act of terrorism. The definitions in no way justify or condemn the act of terrorism. The definitions do not present terrorism as a right or wrong way of addressing grudges; rather the different definitions are a representation of how the various organizations and individuals perceive it. Terrorists themselves might have a different definition of their act. What is called terrorism thus seems to depend on one's point of view (Hoffman, Jenkins).

In his book, *inside terrorism*, Bruce Hoffman observed that terrorism has undergone certain fundamental changes in meaning. He remarked thus, "The word 'terrorism' was first popularized during the French Revolution. In contrast to its contemporary usage, at that time, terrorism had a decidedly positive connotation" (2006).

Federal Bureau of Intelligence (FBI) defines terrorism as the unlawful use of force or violence against persons or property to intimidate or coerce a Government, the civilian population, or any segment thereof, in furtherance of political or social objectives.

The Department of Homeland Security (DHS) defines terrorism as any activity that involves an act that: is dangerous to human life or potentially destructive of critical infrastructure or key resources: and …must also appear to be intended (i) to intimidate or coerce a civilian population; (ii) to influence the policy of a government intimidation or coercion; or (iii) to affect the conduct of a government by mass destruction, assassination, or kidnapping.

Terrorism, according to the Department of Defense, is the calculated use of unlawful violence to inculcate fear; intended to coerce or to intimidate governments or societies in the pursuit of goals that are generally political, religious, or ideological objectives.

In conclusion, terrorism could be defined as the deliberate creation and exploitation of fear through violence or the threat of violence in the pursuit of political change (2006).

From the various definitions, it could be deduced that terrorism is a tool used by an individual or group of disgruntled elements to vent their bottled resentment and express frustration against an establishment's real or perceived injustice. Terrorism in certain circumstances could be targeted at the hapless citizens in order to embarrass their government. It could be directed at government officials for formulating policies not palatable to certain elements in society. At other times, terrorism could be directed towards the destruction of government or individual properties, with the aim to attract attention, garner sympathy and to make a point.

But the fundamental question remains whether or not these acts of terrorism could have been peacefully negotiated before they spiraled out of control.

Acts of terrorism do not just spring from the blues; they are triggered by certain factors: real or imagined. Human beings, not spirits, perpetrate acts of terrorism. But the clandestine nature of terrorism makes it hard for authorities to easily trace their source, and therefore, the reason\s behind terrorism. Some of the reasons people resort to terrorism are as discussed herein.

Injustice

Injustice seems the main reason people engage in terrorism. Injustice means an act that inflicts undeserved hurt. It applies to any act that involves unfairness to another or violation of one's rights (Merriam-Webster dictionary). Terrorism may include acts of violence committed by groups that view themselves as victimized by some notable and powerful nations, groups or even individuals. Terrorism could be a commensurate reaction to acts of oppression, repression or denial of due rights of a people or of an individual by authorities of an establishment.

Frustration

Frustration is a deep chronic sense or state of insecurity and dissatisfaction arising from unresolved problems or unfulfilled needs (*Medical Dictionary*). Any frustrated person is capable of engaging in any form of deadly activity to get even or to communicate a bottled resentment. If, for instance, a government is insensitive to the aspirations of an interest group, this could mark the beginning of conflict between the government and the group. Oftentimes, such conflict breeds terrorism.

Jealousy

Jealousy is resentment against a rival, a person enjoying success or advantage, or against another's success or advantage itself (*Dictionary.com*).

It is factual that some countries are more economically and technologically prosperous than others. In an effort to create their imagined state of equality, a group of individuals might gang up against the prosperous nation. The group might even accuse the nation of contributing to their own woes, hence the justification to embark on property destruction and hostage taking, for ransom, leading to terrorism.

This situation can also trickle down to individuals and local groups. For instance, it is alleged that the Hausa / Fulani group in northern Nigeria feels impoverished by culture and lack of leadership. The dethroned Emir of Kano, Sanusi Lamido, noted as an outspoken critic of governance in the region, blamed leaders for failing to tackle poverty and illiteracy in the region. The monarch believes: We are in denial. The northwest and the north-east, demographically, constitute the bulk of Nigeria's population, but look at human development indices, look at the number of children out of school, look at adult literacy, look at maternal mortality, look at infant mortality, look at girl-child completion rate, look at income per capita, the north-east and the north-west Nigeria, are among the poorest parts of the world (J.C. Moses, Ventures Africa April 18, 2017). To vent their frustration, these individuals – often referred to as Fulani herdsmen – head down south kidnapping and robbing their more perceived and/or real prosperous southerners.

Fanaticism

Fanaticism is the attempt to repress elements of one's own being for the sake of others. If the fanatic encounters these elements in somebody else, he fights against them passionately, because they endanger the success of his own repression (Tillich).

Religious zealots under the guise of defense of their religious beliefs carry out acts of terrorism to intimidate people into accepting their faith. It is noteworthy that no particular religion has the monopoly of fanaticism. Islam has often been wrongly associated with perpetrating terrorism in the name of their belief system. But the truth is that this religion of peace – according to its founder – has been hijacked by fanatics whose mission has nothing to do with proselytization. An example is the Boko Haram group, which terrorizes every city and individual in their trail, irrespective of religious affiliation.

Intimidation

Intimidation is to make timid; fill with fear; to coerce or inhibit by or as if by threats (*The Free Dictionary*).

Government is saddled with the responsibility of protecting its citizenry. And in this regard any credible government arrests and prosecutes violators of the laws of the land. Yet in almost every nation on earth, there exist pressure groups whose whole aim is to protect its members against government oppression. These groups tend to run a parallel government within the government. To influence law enforcement, in order to get away with crime, some groups try to intimidate the government by engaging in acts of terrorism.

Intimidation and embarrassment of government are paramount instruments of terrorism.

Although these groups have no formal connection with governments, they usually have the financial and moral backing of sympathetic governments. Typically, they stage unexpected attacks on civilian targets, including embassies and airliners, with the aim of sowing fear and confusion (*The American Heritage New Dictionary of Cultural Literacy*, 2005).

Shades of terrorism

Hapless individuals and volatile groups tend to take their fate in their hands in the face of official injustice and highhandedness. This becomes necessary because if people do not stand up and defend themselves, the more powerful and influential groups will try to obliterate them. Relationship between the Rohingya people and the state of Myanmar readily comes to mind. It is not yet established that the people of Rohingya have fought back; it is a matter of time before the world rallies to their defense.

Peace-loving, non-violent advocates of human freedom from oppression, intimidation, exploitation, injustice have at certain points accused some government agencies of not believing in peaceful resolution of conflicts. Given this type of situation, terrorism, if targeted at the oppressor, could still not be justified, but capable of winning popular sympathy.

In Syrian, government forces and rebels fight for authority and legitimacy. Rebels, backed by sympathizers and mercenaries, deploy every available military and non-conventional tactic to puncture and deflect the authority of the government. Although the rebels are fighting a legitimate government, their action could be justified by the fact that the government refuses to listen to the people's yearning for change.

Terrorism, anywhere, anytime, on anyone, is condemnable and abhorrent. However, since human beings are created equal, any act that deprives individuals of this God-given equality and freedom must be met with commensurate resistance, including acts of terrorism. No amount of authority justifies the repression of natural human freedom. Therefore, in the event that a tyrannical regime engages in the act of oppression of minorities and the less-privileged in society, the victims have the inalienable right to defend their existence, even if it involves engaging in acts of terrorism against an oppressive regime.

In certain circumstances, suicide attacks have become widespread as an instrument of terrorism. Suicide attack in terrorism is equivalent to gorilla tactic in military warfare - the damage is done before the attacker is detected.

History is replete with instances of simmering conflicts. History of such conflicts will not be complete without the story of frosty relationship between Israel and Palestine. Things came head-on between Israel and Palestine that the out-numbered Palestine was left with little option but to resort to self-help. Increasingly, Palestinians are coming to see suicide attacks as a strategic weapon, a poor man's *smart bomb* that can miraculously balance Israel's technological prowess and conventional military dominance. Suicide bombings give them something no other weapon could: the ability to cause Israel devastating and unprecedented pain (Luft).

As the process of purposely ending one's own life, suicide is viewed differently according to culture and religion. Some societies consider suicide honorable in certain cases, while other societies may treat it as a crime. Some people commit suicide out of frustration and despondency, while others commit suicide to prove their strong faith in their cause.

In certain African cultures, suicide is a taboo, an offense against the gods, neighbors, relatives, and the community as a whole. Such culture views anyone who commits suicide as being possessed by evil forces. Therefore, the victim's remains are not buried like every other dead. The remains are committed to the evil forest without the necessary burial rites. The people believe that the deities are not happy with the dead and, therefore, not deserving of their protection (it is the people's belief that the deities protect both the living and the dead.).

Conversely, elsewhere in the world, suicide could be a heroic act, deserving of praise and the necessary accolade. For instance, Palestinian society lauds martyrs (suicide perpetrators) for their bravery and selflessness. Typically, candy is distributed in the streets and women respond with traditional shrieks of joy (Hoffman).

In Recent years, suicide has become an indispensable instrument of protestation. It has been used in Chechnya and Yugoslavia, Jews and Arabs, Al-qaeda and the United States interests, Boko Haram and Nigerian interests, just to mention a few.

Suicide is known to be cost effective as an instrument of war. Except in the United States, where Bin Laden's extremist group flew planes into the twin towers and the Pentagon, most other ones have only involved individuals adorning the deadly vest. Even at that, it was little cost to the terrorists because the planes were hijacked. America lost human and material, while the suicide perpetrators lost just men, which, in their sponsors' estimation, is a just price to pay for their mission.

The act of suicide as an instrument of war, reprisal, intimidation, oppression, and other sinister missions is cowardice. Some of the perpetrators are young innocent teens that have been brainwashed. Their sponsors hardly undertake such missions themselves. They, like army generals, are the last to die in any warfare. If these 'generals' are not prepared to wear the vests themselves, why do they go about recruiting other people to wear them? If these suicide sponsors have nerves, they should confront their opponents in a more civilized manner. They can either test their military might in an open combat or take their dispute to mediation.

Mediation versus Self-help

Dialogue and mediation remain the most effective means of addressing any concerns. Instead of taking to suicide and other clandestine means of redress, terrorists should openly address the bone of contention in civilized forums. The United Nations has been a big time mediator in international conflicts. Terrorists should first bring their grievances to the world body before venting their frustration on their opponent – if it ever comes to that.

Even at the deadlock of mediation, there is still no justification for suicide bombing. The evil of suicide bombing is quite enormous. It involves taking innocent lives – both of the victims and the (naïve) recruit suicide bomber.

In the civilized world, individuals express their grievances through the court or by bringing them to mediation and arbitration. In the terrorism world, jungle justice reigns. Most acts of terrorism are nocturnal and clandestine. Often, the perpetrators are faceless. Therefore, they hardly express their agitation before carrying out their nefarious attacks.

From their account, terrorists feel that they are unfairly persecuted. As a way of remaining relevant and currying sympathy, they engage in terrorism. An example is a statement credited to the Palestinian terrorist team at the wake of the 1972 Munich Olympic massacre. It states, "We are persecuted people who have no land and no home land...why should the whole world be having fun and entertainment while we suffer with all ears deaf to us?" (Hoffman). The Biafran side also expressed this same sentiment when General Gowan's Nigerian government blockaded food supply, leading to massive starvation and death of children and adults.

Starvation was a Nigerian weapon of war. It broke Biafra. It made Zambia, Tanzania, and Ivory Coast recognize Biafra. It made the International Red Cross call Biafra its gravest emergency since World War II. Britain supplied arms and advice to Nigeria. The Soviet Union sent technicians and planes to Nigeria, thrilled at the chance to influence Africa without offending America or Britain. Communist China denounced the Anglo-American-Soviet imperialism but did little else to support Biafra. The French sold Biafra some arms but did not give the recognition that Biafra most needed. The world, therefore, remained silent while Biafrans died (Adichie). Unlike the Palestinian group, Biafran militia never had the wherewithal and the mindset to hijack planes and terrorize people who had no stake in the conflict between it and Nigeria.

Some terrorist groups see themselves as sent by God to liberate humanity. They believe that their mission is to defeat the enemy – the oppressor – and obtain victory for the common people. This claim has neither always, nor ever, been the case.

Oftentimes, terrorists end up hurting the people they claim to protect.

When the Niger Delta militant groups in Nigeria began their agitation for some share in the oil revenue, many people were sympathetic to their cause. They blew up oil pipelines; sabotaged government interests along the creeks, including commandeering of barges and ocean liners along the coastal region; made the mangrove swamps inaccessible to government forces. They asked people to boycott government activities. They also asked people to revolt against the government. The gullible citizenry complied with the militants' directives. But this compliance lasted for as long as the militants' cause sounded genuine.

As the agitation progressed, criminal elements infiltrated the ranks of the militants. They took hostage of government officials, oil workers and civilians alike. They deviated from their original mission of service to the deprived Niger Deltans and resorted to selfish kidnapping of people for ransom. They engaged in all kinds of atrocities ranging from robbery to rape. They gradually lost their identity as representatives of the deprived and exploited public. The people stopped seeing them as heroes as much as they more and more became the people's nemesis.

A concerned citizen summarized it thus:

When kidnapping was first introduced in the Niger Delta area of Nigeria, it was primarily targeted at expatriates who were accused of plundering the local resources without commensurate royalty to host communities. As the situation further deteriorated, expatriates became so cautious and were nowhere to be found. Therefore, kidnappers resorted to taking hostage of locals who were suspected as being rich. These rich victims were then kidnapped for ransom. What started as a plan to favor local resource owners, thereafter, degenerated into pain and agony for the same people they were meant to save.

Similarly, at the advent of the fanatical group, Boko Haram, in Northeast Nigeria, sympathy by the Muslim community in Nigeria became rife. The group enjoyed a lot of followership for a while. Some topnotch government officials were even alleged to promote the group's cause. Some notable organizations and wealthy Muslim faithful were also accused of complicity in the operations of the shadowy group. The tide, however, started turning against them when they took hostage of students of a government secondary boarding school for girls in Chibok, located in the same self-declared Caliphate. Although the group perpetrated a whole lot of havoc, the climax was the terrorism of the people they were supposed to defend from western influence, as defined by the group.

Some terrorist groups are constant attention-seekers. Insofar as they get publicity, they keep terrorizing the populace. Newsprint and airtime are thus the coin of the realm in the terrorists' mind-set, the only tangible or empirical means they have by which to gauge their success and assess their progress. In this respect, little distinction or discrimination is made between good and bad publicity. The satisfaction of simply being noticed is often regarded as sufficient reward (2007). In the light of this situation, one wonders what such terrorists aim to achieve.

In the commercial world, it is often believed that one's prominence is hinged on the individual's ability to notify the target audience. If individuals keep quiet about their existence, their intended audience will never notice their presence – This is the power of advertising. Terrorists take advantage of media publicity in perpetrating violence. If the media should ignore terrorist activities, there is the likelihood that terrorism will reduce.

Terrorists are described as a small group of individuals living underground, in close proximity to one another, constantly on the run and fearful of arrest and betrayal. Because they are not sure of even one another, they must possess good intelligence. Armed with good intelligence, they are able to decipher activities in and around their camps. They can plan and execute terror undetected.

Osama bin Laden was detected and eliminated having lived in Pakistan for an unspecified number of years. He and his terror group were able to plan and execute terror activities from his residence because he had good intelligence. On the flip side, every piece of *good intelligence* has an expiration date. A little hole along the line of transmission is capable of ruining, in one split second, whole years of planning. This could come in the form of sabotage by an aggrieved member of the group or a concerned member of the civil society – that was probably bin Laden's waterloo.

Terrorists could sometimes be mistaken for spirits. They tend to act in mysterious ways. However, when their network is busted, they are known to be cowards who live under the shadow of a large group whose stock in trade is to instill misery and destruction in society.

Some terror groups might have genuine grudge against their opponent. They either lack the courage to present their issue in a civilized manner or believe they would not be given the desired attention. Since their supposed opponent has no idea what they are agitating for, it is difficult to even discuss with them. Again, some governments believe it is weakness to negotiate with terrorist groups. But if anything we hear in the news is worth the effort, U.S. Central Commander, Gen. Frank McKenzie, was cited to have told lawmakers that the United States had provided *very limited support* to the Taliban in its fight against ISIS in the eastern Afghanistan province of Nangarhar (Katie Williams, Defense One, March 10, 2020). This tends to corroborate Hamid Karzai – then Afghan president's confirmation that the United States government was in a dialogue with the Taliban (Fox News June 18, 2011). If it is factual that a group believed to fraternize with al-Qaeda – a terrorist group – is getting such recognition, it therefore, goes to show that terrorism has come to stay as part of the political spectrum.

Terrorism is not a congenital disease. No one is born a terrorist. Situations force people to resort to terrorism. There is yet no scientific proof that terrorism is in the gene. Osama bin Laden's progeny, for instance, have no business being terrorists if they are not inclined to be. All indices point to the fact that bin Laden's family rose to prominence from the construction industry. There has been no single indication anywhere that bin Laden was from a family that made a living from terrorism. If he were not inclined to become a terrorist, bin Laden would have continued the family's trade – construction. That he took to terrorism does not mean that he inherited it from his father or was born with radicalism in his blood. Something pushed him into it.

Mediation and Terrorism

To effectively mediate in terrorism-related matter, the root cause of their action must be known and addressed. Mediation, like hostage negotiation, is the process of trying to align two often completely polarised parties. Authorities view hostage taking as unacceptable demands made by unacceptable means. Terrorists view their action as completely justified, even on moral and religious grounds. To attempt any reconciliation efforts, it is essential for mediators to understand terrorist culture, their profile, their personality, their view of the world and also the authorities, their values and their framing of the problem raised (Faure, Zartman).

In the history of terrorism mediation, it has not gone without its own human and material costs. This has been for numerous reasons ranging from wrong mediation approach to lack of understanding of the mindset of terrorists.

In the health sector, prescriptions are based on the outcome of prognosis. To correctly diagnose a problem is paramount for its solution. In order, therefore, to secure a meaningful mediation involving terrorists, their grievance must be heard and understood; they must be seen. Their opponent must be willing to discuss the issues objectively. The aggrieved must first be seen as human beings and empathized with. The appellation, *terrorist*, could pose a barrier to mediation. Just as in the law court where defendants should not be addressed as prisoners or criminals until they are convicted and sentenced, so also the aggrieved should not be termed *terrorist* until such a time when incontrovertible evidence has been proven against them.

Conflict is an ill-wind, which blows no good to anyone. Should conflict eventually erupt between two parties, a few options should be on the table in order to attain a peaceful settlement. First, parties should endeavor to know the reason/s behind the action. They should weigh their reason/s for the action with relevant societal norms. The utmost goal should be a determination whether or not such reasons favor the majority of the populace or driven by selfish ambition?

Depending on the parties' disposition, leadership of the aggressive party or its influential figurehead should be identified with the view to establishing detailed audience with them. Representatives of both parties should moderate such meeting. The onus lies on the superior party – if it were a conflict between the government and an aggrieved group – to ensure that the weaker party – even though it were the aggressor, is granted a safe landing, irrespective of the outcome of mediation. The need for this is to encourage others who might nurse grudges against the society to present them in a civilized manner instead of taking the law into their own hands, thereby breed terrorism.

Should a conflict take a political dimension between the government and a splinter group, the president confronted with terrorists' demand for takeover of the government has a few options, excluding immediate roll out of the nation's armament. First approach would be to address their demand by asking them to test their popularity by putting their name on the ballot.

Should their demand be economic in nature, such as the case of the Niger Delta militants and the Nigerian government, mediators are faced with the choice between ameliorating the cause or escalating the conflict. One smart move made by the government of late President Yar'adua of Nigeria was to grant amnesty to the militants who were seeking to control the resources of the region. The government traded the militants' arms for cash and granted their youth scholarships, economically empowered some of them and developed the hitherto neglected region.

Struggle between organized terrorism and the civil society is not easily wished away. It takes patience, diplomacy, tactics, sacrifice, and some measure of humility. When there is a stalemate, parties wait for who will blink first. Someone has to take the initiative. It is the wise and mature party that backs down, not out of weakness, but for peaceful coexistence in society. Peaceful coexistence is absolutely possible in the world if people will patiently listen to each other in mediation.

VII

RELIGION, SPIRITUALITY AND MEDIATION

For any meaningful conflict resolution project, religion and the spirituality of the disputants must be taken into consideration. Mediators must familiarize themselves with the rudiments of religion and spirituality in relation to both the disputants and their bone of contention. This is so that when the disputants express themselves, the mediator will know where they are coming from. The mediator will also understand the disputants' sensitive issues and boundaries.

Since religion is such a diverse phenomenon, different people view it from different angles. For clarity, a few definitions of religion become necessary.

Religion is a set of beliefs concerning the cause, nature, and purpose of the universe, especially when considered as the creation of a superhuman agency or agencies, usually involving devotional and ritual observances, and often containing a moral code Governing the conduct of human affairs (*Dictionary.com Unabridged*).

A snapshot characterizes religion thus:

- ✓ a set of rules that a certain sect of a society abides by
- ✓ a human quest for fundamental answers
- ✓ does teach the followers obedience, humility, self-denial, forgiveness and non-resistance. (Gaikwad).

Religion, from the purview of spiritual psychology, is: A conscious awareness, integration and use of one's situations, health, music, suffering, sickness, death, sports, food, wears, environments, dispositions, achievements, failures, struggles, destinies, education, status, neighbors, friends, enemies, in endless, timeless and perpetual adoration, devotion, thanksgiving and appreciations to one's source of being and life (Nwachukwu).

The relationship between religion and spirituality cannot be overemphasized. Both are close, yet far apart – dependent on applicability.

One can be so religious without mindful of what it means to relate and care for others. It is only when one incorporates good work and behavior with theology that one aspires to spirituality. The qualifying criteria for heavenly rewards are based on being practical and sensitive to the minutest needs of the least of society – the helpless, the outcast, the marginalized, orphans, and those poverty-stricken individuals living in the midst of affluence, having limited means of survival. Truth, justice, equity and spiritual prosperity are positive signs of true spiritual growth as the Creator expects of humanity. A simple theological arithmetic could serve as a guide. The equation stipulates that religion plus good work is equal to eternal success, and good work minus religion is still equal to eternal success. But religion minus good work equals to eternal loss (Nwachukwu).

Both spirituality and religion aim to take an individual towards the ultimate goal of life. Religion provides a set of guidelines, which the faithful must embrace without questions. Often, religious beliefs instill fear of God in adherents and make people do things without questioning the rationale behind their action. Spirituality, on the other hand, leads an individual into self-reflection, helping individuals believe that their being is God's residence, leading to uprightness. Spirituality is an individual experience of the encompassing effect. A spiritual person finds his own way, travels it alone and reaches there in a state of euphoria. Therefore, following a religion is doing a duty, whereas being spiritual is being who you are (Gaikwad).

The relationship between religion and spirituality is as enumerated:

1. Religion and spirituality both refer to man's desire to find inner peace or God, regardless of the terminology they use.
2. Religion employs literature and rituals in its worship whereas spirituality uses personalized prayer and meditation.
3. To an outsider, religion may seem all about ritual while spirituality avoids anything that can become meaningless through repetition.
4. The rituals of religion are meant to foster a community of believers that provide both spiritual and physical succor to its members while people who consider themselves to be only spiritual are generally left to their own devices (Manisha).

Religion, according to Austine Cline, is spiritual and spirituality is religious. One tends to be more personal and private while the other tends to incorporate public rituals and organized doctrines. The lines between one and the other are not clear and distinct —— they are all points on the spectrum of belief systems known as religion. Neither religion nor spirituality is better or worse than the other; people who try to pretend that such a difference does exist are only fooling themselves (Cline,2010).

Having looked at the various aspects of religion, it becomes important that any mediator in any given conflicts must familiarize himself/herself with these definitions and aspects in the event situations arise in the course of mediation whereby they have to decipher the reason/s behind disputant's actions.

Karl Marx, a twentieth century German philosopher, stated that religion is the opium of the people or the opiate of the masses. As an opiate of the masses, religion is an instrument for maintaining social stratification and for keeping the masses under control.

Many an epoch has produced religious gurus as well as religious bigots and zealots, fundamentalists and terrorists. There have been numerous instances where religion has been used as an excuse to exterminate people whose faith differs from the perpetrators'. Numerous examples of such situation exist almost round the globe. They abound between Jews and Muslims; Christians and Animists. There are also such intractable inter-religious wars in Northern Ireland between Catholics and Protestants; Bosnia-Herzegovina, Sudan, Myanmar – the list continues.

The war in Bosnia-Herzegovina, according to *Ontario Consultants on Religious Tolerance*, was among three faith groups, (Muslim, Roman Catholic, and Serbian Orthodox). The Serbian Orthodox Christian attack on Muslims was elevated to the level of genocide (Robinson, 2011).

For the religious terrorist, violence is first and foremost a sacramental act of divine duty executed in direct response to some theological demand or imperative (Hoffman, 2007). Some religious adherents are willing to jump off the Tappan Zee Bridge because their religious leader orders them to, as part of their religious sacrifice. Some religious leaders therefore capitalize on the gullibility of their followers to manipulate their thoughts and actions.

Dr. Martin Luther King, Jr., Nelson Mandela, and a host of other crusaders of civil liberties had series of rallies; yet their mission was devoid of violence. No doubt, there were pockets of skirmishes resulting from those rallies, but the messengers themselves never directly or indirectly tried to instigate the people to terrorize the society. But many a religious leader has at one time or the other incited hatred and violence by the invocation of sections of theological claims to justify their action. Numerous examples abound: Ayatollah Khomeini's declaration of Islamic republic of Iran, 1979. He is quoted as inciting violence (probably inadvertently) when he declared: We must strive to export our revolution throughout the world (Hoffman). This is believed to be at the root of the Iranian-backed Islamic terrorist campaign.

There is an aphorism: Give the dog a bad name to hang it. This is a tactic often employed by terrorist religious groups. Some of these denigrating and dehumanizing name-calling, such as infidels, evil generation, descendants of the devil, and other unprintable names.

It is on record that Osama bin Laden described the bombing of the twin towers in New York on September 11, 2001 as an act of God and as a punishment on "infidel armies" who must "leave the land of Muhammad" - (probably alluding to America's support for Israel and the struggles in Palestine).

Bin Laden was quoted as saying:

He whom God guides is rightly guided but he whom God leaves to stray, for him wilt thou find no protector to lead him to the right way...God Almighty hit the United States at its most vulnerable spot. He destroyed its greatest buildings. Praise be to God (2007).

Although not a religious leader, bin Laden cites a portion of the holy book, to justify his killing of people in American soil, be they Americans or foreigners, Christians, animists, atheists, Muslims or Jews. He stopped at nothing to make America look bad in the eyes of the Islamic world, presenting the United States as an enemy of Islam.

Religious terrorism is traceable to virtually all kinds of human conflicts. The conflict might originally look civil in nature. As it escalates, its religious trappings gradually emerge. The war in Sudan war was originally civil; later it became a conflict between the Muslim north and Christian south. In Nigeria, originally the war was civil, but as it escalated, it became divided between Northern Nigeria Muslims and Biafra Christian south. If the Western world knew what they know

now about religious terrorism, the outcome of the Biafra/ Nigeria war would have been different.

Intolerance breeds injustice. Injustice invariably leads to rebellion and retaliation, and these lead to escalation, making reconciliation almost impossible (Robinson, 1999). This is where mediation and mediators tend to have a bitter taste in their mouth in peacemaking and reconciliation.

The Islamic Faith

It would sound stereotypical to note that there seems to be a culture of violence associated with the Islamic religion. Controversial as this notation is, it is placed here as a scholarly topic to stimulate an academic discourse.

Islam is acclaimed a religion of peace. Therefore, it beats any enlightened imagination to note that a religion, which is founded on peace would witness such spates of violence as seen in the present world events. In defense of the religion, just like every other organization infiltrated by fanatics, Islam has its fair share of fanatics who wrongly interpret and implement certain injunctions. Such radicals have twisted interpretation and understanding of the teachings of Islamic religion that contradict their real meaning. Otherwise, there is no meaningful, peaceful religion, which is expected to deliberately promote and encourage the same amount of violence noticed in areas of the world with large concentration of Muslims.

There are indeed aspects of the Quran that are obviously excerpted out of context or without full context and used as justification for Holy War. One such misinterpreted section of the Islamic Holy Book is as cited below.

"Fight against those who believe not in Allah, nor in the Last Day, nor forbid that which has been forbidden by Allah and His Messenger, and those who acknowledge not the religion of truth among the people of the Scripture, until they pay the Jizyah with willing submission, and feel themselves subdued." (Surah At-Taubah Chapter 9:29).

A closer look at the above passage shows *Allah's messenger* as Prophet Mohammad. The *religion of truth* is Islam. *People of the scripture* in this context are probably Jews and Christians.

This aspect is often cited as justification for attacks on non-Muslim interests. At other times, fanatical preachers incite religious adherents to violence. One example is an influential Nigerian Islamic Cleric, Sheik Ahmad Abubakar Gumi, who at various times had made inflammatory remarks capable of inciting fanatics against non-Muslims. He was once quoted as being in odds with the idea that there was a plot to oppress Muslims since the Chief of Army Staff was a non-Muslim (Enyiagu, 2012). This came at the peak of Boko Haram menace during the administration of President Goodluck Jonathan whose army chief was General Ihejirika (rtd), a southern Christian. This situation emboldened the marauding terrorists in the northeast.

Any fanatic could capitalize on this statement to cause consternation among a hitherto peaceful government. Since Nigeria and Biafra fought a brutal thirty-month civil war, there has been a somewhat mutual distrust between people of various ethnic groups in the once united country. The army seems an exclusive preserve of the predominantly Muslim north. Army leadership has always come from the north. But for the first time, the leadership swings to a southern Christian, giving rise to the likes of Sheik Gumi's vituperation.

Islam does not recognize a distinction between sacred and profane or between spiritual and temporal realms. Islam, therefore, molds the life of individuals and structures of a social order so that the kingdom of God may be promoted on earth. This could be cited as the reason behind the cleric's assertion. Because in a society where there is a clear demarcation between religion and politics, whoever becomes the army chief is immaterial. The constitution should be the reference point as opposed to any individual whims and caprices by either the head of state or an official of the state.

Prophet Mohammad founded Islam. As the founder of the movement he obviously assumed the religious and political leadership, known as the Caliph. In reality, therefore, "many Muslims argue that, unlike Christianity, Islam does not separate religion from state and a majority of Muslims around the world welcome a significant role for Islam in their countries' political life". (L.A. Times, December 5, 2010).

In Islam, the Fatherhood of God lays a foundation for Islamic Brotherhood. The Fatherhood of God is implemented by the ancestral fatherhood of Adam (Sura 4:11; 49:13). Islam also teaches that mankind was a single nation from the beginning (Sura 2:213). Brotherhood has been made a Supreme ideal and it has enabled Islam to reconcile elements of race, ethnicity, custom and culture. As a result, brotherhood has been given due prominence in the interpersonal relationships.

Fanatics often misconstrue this aspect of the Islamic holy book to mean that everybody must belong to one religion, since mankind comes from one source and belong to one God. This oneness is superficial in application and only in principle. Every individual will never belong to one religion either by hook or crook.

The State Department described Al-Qaida as a terrorist organization existing as a sub-cultural group in the Middle Eastern Islamic community. According to the group's founder, Usama Bin Ladin, its main goal is to establish a pan-Islamic Caliphate throughout the world by working with allied Islamic extremist groups to overthrow regimes it deems *non-Islamic* and expelling Westerners and non-Muslims from Muslim countries (terrorismfiles.org, 2012).

Al-Qaida, since its establishment in the late 1980s has increased in scope and strength. It was initially started to bring together Arabs who fought in Afghanistan against the Soviet invasion. In recent years, numerous terrorist acts have been directly or indirectly linked to it. The climax of these terrorism acts was the hijacking and flying of airplanes into the World Trade Center, New York, on September 11, 2001.

The allied military forces fighting in the Persian Gulf were not only confronted with faceless local militia, they also grappled with religious interest groups. Al-Qaida whose primary agenda is the protection of Islam feels violated and insulted because the *invading forces* have not operated according to the dictates of Islamic religion. The United Nations, on the other hand, steps up pressure to get the splinter groups to support the governments of the day to fight international terrorism. These divergent views give rise to lingering conflicts in some

Arab countries. The result is that international efforts aimed at mediation in conflicts in these areas are stifled and almost impossible.

Throughout history, religion, has inadvertently or deliberately lent itself to aggression, hostility and brutality in order to remain relevant. Some of the reasons given for such hostility include heresy and apostasy by the so-called infidels. Jihads have been organized in the past to counter the infidels. At other times, crusades by other religions were organized for this same purpose.

In the words of President Barack Obama, "Unless we get on our high horse and think this is unique to some other place, remember that during the Crusades and the Inquisition, people committed terrible deeds in the name of Christ." The seemingly innocuous statement made at an annual National Prayer Breakfast earned him an earful.

As if religion has lost its original aim, its practitioners often tend to perpetrate all forms of social ills in the guise of religion.

In his discussion about the African predicament, George Ehusiani observes:

> In countries where religious clashes have not taken the dimension of a full-scale war there have been at least hundreds of lives lost to sporadic religious skirmishes. The result of all these is that human life is becoming increasingly cheaper by the day. Human blood is beginning to lose its traditional sacredness, because it is so frequently spilled for the

flimsiest of reasons, while the awe traditionally associated with corpses is disappearing (1991).

The constitution of most democratic governments clearly specifies a difference between religion and politics (Jefferson, 1789). Till this day, this remains the charter governing most western governments. But this is not the same case with some Arab states. Therefore, any attempt by the West to intervene or mediate in conflicts in the Arab states is susceptible to suspicion of an imposition of democratic ideals.

To forestall this situation, Hope rightly cautioned:

We imposed our own values upon the Iraqi people, hoping that giving them a democratically elected government would automatically stabilize their interactions. However, because they themselves did not directly seek this ... they had no model to help them learn how to live in democracy. One major flaw with this model is that this *strange system of government* would eventually be a sufficient reason to resort to violence in order to right the wrongs or "to make things feel *normal* again" (2008).

No matter how much western countries try to play religious neutrality – that is the claim of secularism – they cannot deny the high prevalence of Christianity in their mediation efforts in the Middle East. This being the case, therefore, it would be practically impossible for the international community to successfully mediate in conflicts in the Middle East. "Middle Eastern people, to a large extent, think collectively about issues that challenge their culture. They often make decisions based on ... what their local mosque dictates...." (Hope).

Sharia regulates all religious, political, and social affairs. Islamic legislations cover all aspects of human affairs: food, drinks, intoxicants, meat, dress, business, inheritance, administration, et cetera.

In Islam, a religious heretic or rebel risks execution, crucifixion, or maiming of some organs of the body or be exiled (Sura 5:36). For a thief, the punishment is the chopping off of the hand (Sura 5:41).

Sura 2:178 stipulates thus:

> In the cases of murder, the free for the free,
> The slave for the slave,
> The woman for the woman...

This is known in Islam as the law of equality, because criminals are punished according to the Koranic law of retaliation.

Note that in Islam a political role is religious obligation. This is the reason every political office holder must have an adequate knowledge of Islamic laws.

To, therefore, plan any meaningful mediation in conflicts in the Arab world, prominence must be given to the Islamic religion and its operations. Transfer of values should by all means be avoided, realizing that what works in a secular state may not work in a strictly Islamic setting.

VIII

REVOLUTION AND CONFLICT DE-ESCALATION

Thus far, popular revolution in the Arab world claimed the leadership of three heads of state: Egypt, Tunisia and Yemen. It also cost the life of one head of state and ruler of Libya. The agitations and struggles are not showing any signs of abatement. In Libya the average citizen is yet to come to terms with the demise of their former long-term despot. Egypt, on the other hand, has since moved to another phase of the revolution. Two of their former leaders have been in and out of prison. Mohammed Morsi was sentenced to death, while Hosni Mubarak died of supposedly natural causes.

The popular revolution that swept parts of the Arab world in recent memory took several forms, often turning violent. While some countries accepted reform, others were not susceptible to the turn of events. These governments, therefore, believed that the agitators were terrorists, because they harassed legally constituted governments. On the part of the agitators, they were simply reclaiming their mandate (if there were any in the first place) from *power usurpers*. They, therefore, believed that their action did not constitute terrorism.

A couple of rhetorical questions may help clarify certain, hitherto, misconceived scenarios. Does every violent, anti-establishment, protest constitute an act of terrorism? For instance, when Palestinians agitate for the creation of a separate state, and to buttress their demand, take hostage of Jewish residents, are they engaging in terrorism? Does Israeli's violent response to such action constitute terror attack? Again, when Catholics and Protestants clash in Northern Ireland, are they terrorizing each other? When the Niger Delta militants take hostage of oil workers in the creeks of Nigeria, to demand an equitable distribution of oil wealth, are they rightly classified as terrorists?

The above situations almost always involve loss of lives and destruction of state and individual properties. The perpetrators of these acts might describe themselves as 'freedom fighters' or liberators of the oppressed' or 'individuals-against-injustice'. On the other hand, government sources may likely classify them terrorists.

The credible argument against these agitators is, like in terrorism, the central issue involves some clandestine activities aimed mainly at an establishment. These activities are often deadly, while at other times, they could be just mere harassment of the civil populace in order to embarrass their government. Often times, these individuals place unrealistic demands on the government. Like terrorists, some of these protesters are unidentifiable. Since no meaningful government will be willing to share power with a faceless group, government sources quickly tag such activities as terrorism, giving it a good reason to clamp down on them.

In recent years, the Nigerian government and a, hitherto, fanatical religious group known as Boko Haram have been having a running battle. This group's modus operandi takes the form of destruction of lives and property, bombing of worship places and other public buildings, including the United Nations building in the capital city of Abuja. In their bid to eradicate western education, the group later abducted nearly three hundred high school girls in the North East of Nigeria. Some of the girls escaped from their captives, some died in the process; yet some were sold as slaves and war bounty to their captives. Government agencies successfully negotiated the release of a handful of the girls. The same scenario repeated itself at another girls' high school in another town in the same region. Again, government successfully negotiated the release of some of the girls. One prominent name: Leah Shuaibu – a Christian who refused to renounce her religion as part of the government deal – was left in captivity.

The Nigerian government tried, in vain, to identify the leaders of the group so they could negotiate. The group claimed that it would only negotiate if the government could extend a similar amnesty as accorded the Niger Delta militants. Niger Delta militants started the whole idea of hostage taking in Nigeria. Their agitation was based on resource control of oil revenue from the region. At the onset of their agitation, Niger Delta militants vowed to cripple the nation's economy. They blew up oil pipelines and expelled oil workers from the region. Government forces indiscriminately arrested the militants. Such arrests further infuriated their sympathizers who formed splinter groups in furtherance of the agitation for the development of the region. Government later realized that the only way out of the mess was to negotiate with the militants and to grant amnesty to the prosecuted militants. Notable mediators stepped in between the government and the militants before issues were discussed and some measure of resolution reached.

Boko Haram militants' claim of amnesty is based on the elimination of anything western, including western education. The Nigerian government tried to exercise restraint due to the sensitive nature of issues bordering on religion in a country already polarized along religious and ethnic lines. This restraint was, however, shelved when the group started occupying territories, hoisting their flag and attacking people irrespective of religious affiliation. It then dawned on the government that the conflict had gone beyond religious coloration. Government strategy changed, and commensurate treatment was accorded the impending security threat.

The unanswered question remains whether the two groups deserve equal and similar form of amnesty considering the reasons for their agitation as well as their threat to peace and security of the country. These are good examples of unsettled agitation for attention and the need for conflict de-escalation.

The Arab Spring And Conflict De-Escalation

Frustration with closed, corrupt, and unresponsive political systems has led to defections among elites and the fall of once powerful regimes in Tunisia, Egypt, and Libya (Goldstone, 2011). Of the three countries mentioned, Tunisia's Ben Ali seemed to heed the call and decided to literally live to fight another day. His temporary resistance was a reasonable human response to a sudden momentary occurrence. He, however, caved in to pressure when he realized that he was getting isolated as the day went by. He was a smart man because he was kicked out of office, went into exile and continued his life instead of going to the great beyond like his contemporary, Quaddafi of Libya, who clung to power till death did him part.

Ben Ali's nemesis was Mohamed Bouazizi, a Tunisian street food vendor, initially wrongly said to be a college graduate. He set himself on fire on 17 December 2010 in protest of the confiscation of his wares and the harassment and humiliation that he reported was inflicted on him by a municipal official and her aides. When the smoke settled, neither Bouazizi, President Zine el-Abidine Ben Ali nor the entire Arab world had an inkling that that singular act of frustration, and to an extent, heroism, would result to a worldwide outrage, spreading like a summer wildfire to even the, hitherto, peaceful areas of the world.

Ben Ali had known crises in the past. He once engaged in anti-French, pro-independence activity, acted as a runner between local Neo-Destour – a liberal, constitutional political party, activists and members of guerrilla bands. When his Neo Destour activities came to the attention of the French colonial administration, Zine Ben Ali was expelled from school and denied admittance to any French-administered school in the colony.

He later assumed the presidency of Tunisia from his prime minister position. He was alleged to have removed the aged, ill

Habib Bourguiba from the presidency, citing mental infirmity as the main reason for his action (Gale, 2006).

Unlike Ali who abdicated, Muammar al-Qaddafi of Libya probably believed he was invincible. He came to power in September of 1969 after a coup against King Idris who was away for a medical treatment in Turkey. He exited power through a bloody and popular uprising culminating in his death. After more than four decades in power, Qaddafi's downfall happened in less than a year (A&E Television Networks, 2012).

Qaddafi was probably a strong man, but his handling of the rebellion against his government was shabby, shameful and unbefitting of an intelligent leader. During the campaign against his government, he was seen at several rallies and in company of a retinue of guards, various security men and women armed to the teeth. He would yell and curse and threaten fire, hell and brimstone. If his aim was to intimidate his opponents, it rather worked against him. When they came for him, he was slaughtered like a festival ram.

Hosni Mubarak ruled Egypt between 1981 after the assassination of Anwar al-Sadat (former president) to 2011, when the Arab Spring swept him off the grips of power.

In Egypt, said Merlyna Lim (a scholar of social transformation at Arizona State University), people shared a yearning to oust Hosni Mubarak, but each person was afraid to step forward. Once they saw how many other Egyptians agreed with them, they grew bolder (Saletan, 2011).

On January 25, 2011, Egyptian protesters began staging large-scale demonstrations throughout the country calling for Mubarak's resignation. The Arab Spring sought to remove dictators across the Middle East and the demonstrators in Cairo's Tahrir Square quickly gained international attention. Though aggressive actions by the protesters were rare at the start, violence in the streets quickly escalated between Mubarak supporters and the opposition following his announcement on February 1 that though he would not resign from the presidency, he also would not seek another term in the elections scheduled for September 2011 (Bard, Berman, Dawson, Scheinerman, Snider).

If his intention for such announcement was to appease the people, he rather infuriated them the more. Shortly after the announcement, Egyptians became more resolute in getting rid of his despotic government. Finally, he yielded to pressure and abdicated, and was later committed to a prison term. His sons were also prosecuted for corruption. Mubarak later passed on.

Ali Abdullah Saleh of Yemen also had a bitter taste of the Arab Spring. He was lucky to get away with just an injury when Yemeni protestors attacked his presidential palace. He was forced to flee to Saudi Arabia. Through high-powered mediation, coupled with a good measure of political gerrymandering, he considered it expedient to hand over power to his deputy.

He (Saleh) made his way up the military's ranks and waited for his opportunities. In 1974, Ibrahim al-Hamdi, with Saleh's help, led a military coup that exiled President Abd-el Rahman al Iryani. Al-Hamdi was murdered in 1977. His successor was assassinated the following year. Saleh had worked with both. On July 17, 1978, Yemen's 99-member People Council elected Saleh president with 76 votes (Tristam, 2012).

Saleh could be adjudged as wise as his Tunisian counterpart. He yielded to pressure and resigned or was kicked out. He was lucky to be living, but not in the presidential mansion.

Bashar al-Assad took over power in Syria at the death of his father. Bashar was originally trained as an ophthalmologist. His medical career came to an abrupt end when his older brother, who was groomed for the presidency, died in an apparent accident.

Since coming in to power, Syrians and the rest of the world have been watching him very closely to see if Assad will follow in the footsteps of his father, a shrewd and uncompromising man who ruled Syria for nearly 30 years with an iron fist (*Encyclopedia Of World Biography, 2004*).

The direction of the Syrian revolution is not yet clear. What seems clear is the people's voice calling for the president's resignation. When similar voices were raised in other parts of the Arab region, the final outcome was in favor of the people who lived after the dust cleared to tell the story.

In Bahrain, the Sunni Al-Khalifa dynasty has ruled since 1820, emboldened by an informal treaty signed with Great Britain granting the Al-Khalifa the official title of Rulers of Bahrain (Mihlar, Eastwood).

The political imbroglio in Bahrain is not abating any time soon. The conditions, which gave rise to the advent of the crisis, are practically institutionalized. For instance, there were claims that the protests were a direct reflection of the political marginalization and discrimination the Shia community faced. It was also a result of the lack of reform and the fact that the dominant group has clung to power for life, to the detriment of the other groups, which consider themselves edged out of the national polity.

According to the Bahrain Center for Human Rights, Shia villages have higher levels of poverty and unemployment than Sunni villages. The protests in Bahrain were not targeted at the leadership as much as on the system that has institutionalized a particular dynasty. Bahrain might sometime in the future find an internal solution to an externally influenced conflict.

To demonstrate that the Arab Spring was no respecter of territories, it even spread beyond the borders of the region of origin and gave rise to other demonstrations against opulence, social and economic inequalities as in the case of *Occupy Wall Street* and other *Occupy* projects elsewhere in the world. Even sacred institutions as the British and Saudi monarchies were not spared.

Perhaps the Saudi Arabian King Abdullah was the smartest of the Arab rulers. Reports had it that his swift reaction to brewing protests saved the kingdom from Arab Spring embarrassments. But his perspicacity did not come without a price. At the notice of local agitations, inspired by protests in other Arab countries, the monarch unveiled $37 billion in benefits for citizens in an apparent bid to curb dissent (Laessing, 2011).

"Death to the dictator" rent the air as protesters in Iran got frustrated with President Mahmoud Ahmadinejad. Ahmadinejad, who has been a taunt on the flesh of some Western powers, seemed unperturbed by the protests. To him, he had seen worst situations and had even been alleged to have taken part in the hostage taking at the American embassy in Tehran. The allegation was vehemently denied.

Some of the former hostages have identified him as one of the student leaders involved in holding 52 American embassy employees for 444 days between 1979 and 1981. Ahmadinejad denies this, as do several of his political opponents who were involved in the embassy take over.

Although the Arab Spring did not immediately sweep the government of Ahmadinejad, Western governments' imposition of sanctions was intended to make or mar the Islamic republic.

Iraq's Saddam Hussein – Some popular understanding is that if it could happen to Saddam Hussein, it could happen to just about any despot. Iraq's Saddam Hussein and his protégé were gone long before the wave of conflicts in the Arab region. Of course, the history of modern conflicts would not be complete without a mention of Iraq, because Iraq endured similar or worst fate, which drove the entire region to mass protests.

In the aftermath of Operation Desert Storm, the United States tacitly encouraged Kurds and Shiites to rebel against Hussein's regime, then withdrew and refused to support them, leaving an unknown number to be slaughtered. At one point, Hussein's regime killed as many as 2,000 suspected Kurdish rebels every day. Some two million Kurds hazarded the dangerous trek through the mountains to Iran and Turkey, hundreds of thousands dying in the process (Rosenberg, 2012).

That was only a minute fraction of crimes against humanity as ascribed to Hussein. He got away with all these atrocities at the watchful gaze of the civilized world. When world leaders eventually woke up from their deep slumber, they, like a drunken gunman, started shooting sporadically in the air, looking for probable reason to indict Saddam and in the process started a situation that worsened the lots of Iraqi people.

Even those opposed to his brutality believe that Iraq was more peaceful when Saddam was ruling. Various Iraqi citizens, young and old, poor and rich, ruling elite and the proletariats alike have expressed this nostalgic sentiment at various points. According to Abbas Mehdi, a former advisor to Iraqi Prime Minister, Nouri al-Maliki, "It was much better in prewar times than today. In terms of security, Saddam Hussein was a criminal. But at least people used to go out, the schools were open (Bruno, 2007).

When the United States government decided to attack Iraq, little did they envisage the resultant devastating effect of the conflict. Prelude to this attack was the annexation in 1990 of Kuwait by Iraqi forces. It should be recalled that the United Nations Security Council Resolutions 660 and 662 condemned Iraq's invasion and annexation and called for the immediate and unconditional withdrawal of Iraqi forces. These resolutions were subsequently followed by a response by the United States *National Security Directive 45*, outlining U.S. objectives: the immediate, complete, and unconditional withdrawal of all Iraqi forces from Kuwait (Richelson, 2001). This was the advent of *Operation Desert Storm*, which president Saddam tagged *mother of all battles*.

A few years later, the United States invaded Iraq, accusing it of stockpiling weapons of mass destruction as well as sponsoring terrorist groups. This culminated in the hanging of Saddam Hussein and a lingering conflict in the Persian Gulf.

From all enlightened indications, it seemed that the main reason the United States went to war in Iraq was to eliminate the oppressive regime of Saddam Hussein. In the same vein, it looked like the charges against the regime were trumped up – a case of giving the dog a bad name to hang it. The various governments of the so-called allies, sooner than later, realized that contrary to their reasons for going to war, the intelligence report was faulty in the first place.

Within the same period in question, Afghanistan became another military target of the United States. This attack was not as surprising as the one on Iraq. While Afghan government was accused of harboring terrorists who launched attacks on the United States, Iraqi government was believed to possess weapons of mass destruction and sponsoring terrorism: unfounded and false allegations. At least President Bush himself would later acknowledge, "…the biggest regret of all the presidency has to have been the intelligence failure in Iraq" (Goldenberg, 2008).

Tony Blair, whose regime as British Prime Minister, waged war against Iraq had some reservation regarding his choice of war over mediation in Iraq. He admitted failing to foresee the *nightmare* that unfolded after he committed British troops to the conflict in 2003 (Blake, 2010).

Before going to war in Iraq, reputable world leaders warned against the idea. Both political and religious leaders voiced their condemnation of the unjust war. One such warning was by Pope John Paul II who spoke out against a possible war in Iraq.

War is not always inevitable. It is always a defeat for humanity. War is never just another means that one can choose to employ for settling differences between nations. War cannot be decided upon, except as the very last option and in accordance with very strict conditions, without ignoring the consequences for the civilian population both during and after the military operations (Cline, 2012).

On March 21, 2003, a nonprofit, progressive, nonpartisan, political activist online site published a litany of condemnations of the war in Iraq.

- Then French president, Jacques Chirac, was credited with saying that France regrets this action undertaken without the approval of the United Nations.
- President Vladimir Putin of Russia described the US-led offensive as a serious political mistake and called for an immediate halt to hostilities.
- Then German Chancellor, Gerhard Schroeder, called war a defeat for politics and said a bad decision was taken.
- China, a UN Security Council permanent member, also opposed to war, appealed to the relevant countries to stop the use of military force.

➤ India, another nuclear power, called the US-led attack a violation of the UN Charter.
➤ Then Mexican president, Vicente Fox, stated: We are against the war.
➤ Then Prime Minister Jean Chretien of Canada called the war unjustified.

In the Middle East, the Palestinian Authority strongly condemned the military campaign. Arab states, Jordan and Saudi Arabia said they were worried about the conflict in the region. In Beirut, then Lebanese President Emile Lahoud warned: We see this aggression today plunging the world into a tunnel where one cannot see the end. In Turkey, then President Ahmet Necdet Sezer, in consonance with the vast majority of Turks voiced opposition to the US-led war.

Then United Nations Secretary General, Kofi Annan, urged the United States and Britain to do everything possible to protect civilians from undue harm and suffering during their campaign to unseat Saddam (Brown, Queally, Germanos, Zimet, Shaughnessy). These warnings point to the fact that in a well-mediated conflict, war may not even be in the horizon, irrespective of the amount of provocation.

In conflict resolution, the mediator assists the disputants to move into the *noetic dimension*. This is where they are able to engage each other with intentionality and creativity in solving their problem, based on their ethical sensitivity, activation of conscience, understanding of values, and search for meaning (Chan). The US-led war in Iraq and other places would have been better prosecuted if the disputants had patiently engaged the services of seasoned mediators.

One major function of mediation is conflict de-escalation, which is synonymous with peacemaking. That being the case, therefore, peacemakers are expected, at all times and at all levels, to maintain their neutrality in order to achieve the desired success in the resolution of conflicts. However, numerous examples abound to seriously wonder whether selective neutrality is widespread in worldwide conflicts.

Charles Taylor, a warlord turned president of Liberia, was accused of instigating conflict on the West coast of Africa. Nigerian government stepped up to mediate. As part of the mediation, Taylor was granted asylum in Nigeria. He had hardly settled down in his new residence before the International Community accused him of causing trouble from his home in southern Nigerian. As a result, the Nigerian government was coerced into sending him packing. In the process of leaving Nigeria, he was arrested and consequently flown to The Hague, where he was tried and is serving time in prison. Charles Taylor – though not a saint – was given a raw deal. Transparency of both president Olusegun Obasanjo Nigerian government and the International Community was doubtful in this case. They seemed to have prearranged his arrest. Taylor deserved to face justice, but to trick him into initial effort towards mediation was unconscionable.

Mr. Taylor probably had his chance at the trial, but the initial treatment leading up to the trial and subsequent conviction clearly manifested a denial of the exercise of his ethical sensitivity, activation of conscience, understanding of values, and search for meaning. A worthwhile mediation helps the parties in a dispute to discover the wisdom, which they brought to the mediation, and to articulate it.

The Arab Spring, an uprising that began in Tunisia in December 2010 changed the political, religious, and cultural face of the Middle East (Blight, Pulham, & Torpey). Consequently, the following year 2011 saw a flurry of activities around North Africa and the Middle East and beyond. These activities graduated from a one-man street protest, which culminated in self-immolation of a Tunisian man, to a generational upheaval, taking its toll on human and material resources. The resultant revolutionary protests and strikes snowballed into what is now a movement that is continuing to remold the societal structure of this region and the entire regions of the world.

The Arab Spring was previously used beginning in March 2005 by numerous media commentators to suggest that a spin-off benefit of the invasion of Iraq would be the flowering of Western-friendly Middle East democracies (Rifai, 2011). If the West and the Middle East have become such sweet hearts, it is only in their hearts. The practicality of such alliance is yet to be felt in their politcal and bilateral relationships.

Various interest groups and individuals have tried to formulate titles for the situation in the region. Some of those titles include the following: Arab Awakening, Arab upheaval, Arab revolution, Arab conflict, Arab uprising. Of all the titles, one thing is common: it is regional. Little wonder why one of those interest individuals remarks thus:

I prefer to call it the Arab upheaval or the Arab uprising. The reason for that is that it is genuinely Arab. It's not something that's happening country by country. It's happening across the entire region simultaneously, with everybody really intensely conscious of the regional nature of it (Lynch, 2012).

The term, Arab Spring, is so called because most of the protests targeting Arab despotic rulers took place or started around and about spring. Since spring comes after winter, this alludes to the fact that weeding out corrupt despots is likened to shedding of leaves in winter, followed by springing of new leaves. The new leaves analogy implies the rise of new leaderships. If the name were *Arab Hurricane*, it would possibly be so violent that no new leaders would survive in such environment. But the idea is not to eliminate all forms of leadership; for a society without meaningful leadership is bound to fail. It was rather an effort aimed to eliminate despotic leaders and supplant them with more malleable and people-friendly ones.

The emotions that motivated the people to create this revolution against the oppressive tyrannies reflect the same force of conflict resolution that drives the goals of mediation. For to stand up and expect to be heard equally and respected accordingly, is the main ingredient in successful resolution of disputes. Mediation in the Middle East must, therefore, take cognizance of the fact that the various parties to the Arab Spring must freely express themselves so that lasting peace could hold sway in the region and beyond.

Conflict Analysis

This study is aimed at an in-depth analysis of the revolution, otherwise known as the Arab Spring. The main characters in the theater, mainly the deposed leaders and their antagonists have contributed in the events leading to rewriting of human history. One question, which seeks sincere and conscientious response, remains whether the international community would have done anything differently to produce a different result. Some interest groups have blamed the international community for undue delays in responding to conflicts in the Middle East. Others have accused western countries of complicity in the Arab revolution. Who is right and wrong is not part of the discussions in this work. However, a look at the appropriateness or otherwise of interventions of the western world in the Arab conflicts will feature prominently herein.

Could the United Nation's mediation have made the outcome of the Arab Spring and the lives of the people any better? Does international mediation really matter in the face of crises? Did the leaders of the various countries ignore signs of the impending crises and the possibility of employing experienced experts in mediation to try defusing tensions prior to the Arab Spring? These are some of the relevant questions addressed in the course of this work.

Arab Spring, for the purpose of this work, is not limited to the revolutionary events of winter 2010 in Tunisia to Summer 2011 in Libya, involving a vendor in Tunisia and a head of state in Libya. The study dates back to pre-independence years of certain countries of the region as well as of some sub-Sahara African countries. Past and recent efforts by the international community aimed at peaceful mediation around the region are also discussed.

The Arab Spring has enjoyed popular acceptance and support from numerous progressive groups and individuals. However, not everyone is on board in matters relating to the situation in the Middle East. One such seeming dissenting voice was that of a former worker with the Central Intelligence Agency and United States State Department's Office of Counter Terrorism who remarks:

> Hosni Mubarak was not a thug ... he was a cooperating partner with the United States in helping secure the border of Israel and pursuing a peace agreement with Israel.... Furthermore, he was in the forefront of battling Islamic extremists in Egypt.... When the protests broke out in Cairo he had every right to expect the United States to have his back. We bolted and abandoned him. And this has set off a chain reaction. Despots and strongmen in Saudi Arabia, Yemen and Bahrain now find themselves no longer able to rely on the United States. So it should not come as a surprise that these folks start pursuing their own survival.... (Johnson, 2012).

From the foregoing, it is indicative that "to have his back" in this context may have meant to mediate in the conflict. Similarly, "pursuing their own survival" likely meant to fight back. This points to the fact that an early and timely mediation would have saved some, if not all, of these precarious situations in the Arab world. An example is the situation in Syria. And the more the outside world sits idly by as Syrians are slaughtered, the more the Sunnis in Syria will believe that the world turns a blind eye to such horrors because of their religion (Cagaptay, 2012).

The whole attempt at formulating a title for conflicts in the Arab region has captured attentions of notable concerned individuals and organizations. Numerous authors have suggested titles and argued against other writers' suggestions. In his own argument, James L. Gelvin asserts, "Springtime has always been associated with renewal, so perhaps it was inevitable that the Arab uprisings would earn the title *Arab Spring*." Buttressing his position, he questioned, "Considering the track record of that Arab spring, why would anyone want to burden the Arab uprisings with this title?"

Arab Spring, would not be his choice of title for the events in the Arab world for two reasons:

> First, the term spring implies a positive outcome for the uprisings, which has yet to be achieved. Second, only one of the uprisings – Syria – actually broke out in that season (if one includes all of March in spring). The others began in the dead of winter, a season hardly appropriate for an uplifting title (Gelvin, 2012).

On the genesis of the Arab Spring, various opinions have been advanced. One popular one is that the revolt was a result of a despairing Tunisian fruit vendor named Mohamed Bouazizi *who* took one way out, setting himself on fire to protest the injustices of the status quo... "THE REVOLT was a settlement of accounts between the powers that be and populations determined to be done with despots" (Fouad, 2012).

Arab Spring was, and continues to be, debated as the title of this movement. The description of this movement "Arab Spring" is continuing to evolve – it may best be defined with the inclusion of appropriate mediation techniques – that would enhance its ability to stimulate positive growth, as opposed to negative perpetuation of conflict.

IX

CONFLICT RESOLUTION AND LEADERSHIP

At various epochs, various parts of the world have had some encounters with all kinds of leaders, ranging from the benevolent to the most malevolent. Civil societies all over the world have at one point or another protested and agitated for change of leadership. In recent memory, the Arab Spring protests seemed the most organized and successful. Another well-organized and executed protest remains the Black Lives Matter movement in the United States. This is attributable to the advent of social networks and the universal consciousness that leadership is supposed to be transient.

This study showcases a couple of past leaders and leadership styles. These are randomly picked to build a case for different concepts of leadership and their relevance and possible comparison to modern day leaders. They do not represent the best or worst leaders. They are not chosen based on their heroism, valor, or even their failings. They are simply picked for contributing to world historical facts. In no particular order, they are discussed below.

Martin Luther King, Jr.

Dr. King's name is synonymous with the American civil rights movement. Advocating a nonviolence approach, King sought equality for African Americans, the economically disadvantaged and victims of injustice through peaceful protest.

In his popular 'prophecy', declared at the steps of the Lincoln Memorial, he shared his dream of a future for all American citizens. King proclaimed,

> This nation will rise up and live out the true meaning of its creed:
> We hold these truths to be self-evident, that all men are created equal.

It is noteworthy that Lincoln was the president who brought down the institution of slavery in the United States. It was thus against the segregation and injustice occasioned by slavery that Dr. King fought and died. History also has it that Lincoln, the 16th President of the United States, was assassinated by an actor and a sympathizer of confederacy and slavery, John Wilkes Booth of Bel Air, Maryland.

During the struggle for equality and desegregation, human rights were violated, resulting in conflicts and tension in society. Through the instrumentality of Dr. King's peaceful civil disobedience and civil rights struggle, peace finally prevailed. Though he was peaceful in his agitation, his opponents were not.

Standing on the balcony of a motel in Memphis where he traveled to support a sanitation workers' strike, King was fatally shot on April 4, 1968. His legacy lives on, even though the world is still subtly racially segregated. Recent protests in America and the whole world stand to testify that King's fight was not over with his death.

Nelson Mandela

"He knew when to compromise. Yet he never compromised his principles. He was a militant. Yet a militant who knew how to plan, assess concrete situations and emerge with rational solutions to problems." —Nelson Mandela.

Boycott, strike, civil disobedience and non-cooperation with policy goals of full citizenship, redistribution of land, trade union rights, and free and compulsory education for all children. These were some of the methods adopted by the African National Congress (ANC) to redress oppression in apartheid South Africa.

Mandela grew up to learn that the African people lived in relative peace until the coming of the white people. He was smart to understand that the children of South Africa had previously lived as one united people, a unity which white men had shattered since settling there. He observed that while black men shared their land, air and water with whites, white men took all of these things for themselves, oppressing the original owners of the land.

Even in the midst of this oppression, Mandela was credited with directing a campaign of peaceful, nonviolent defiance against the South African government and its racist policies.

Mandela influenced the transformation of ANC into a mass grassroots movement, deriving strength from millions of rural peasants and working people who had no voice under the apartheid and white dominated regime.

The oppressive regime that could no longer tolerate Mandela's audacity finally brought him to trial and sentenced him to life imprisonment for political offenses, including sabotage.

He rejected every effort to get him to bargain for his release. He was eventually released after serving twenty-seven years in prison. About one year after his release from prison, he became the leader of the powerful African National Congress, ANC. He subsequently was inaugurated as the country's first democratically elected black president on May 10, 1994, at the age of 77.

Unlike other civil liberty agitators, Nelson Mandela was not killed. On December 5, 2013, at the age of 95, he died at his home in Johannesburg, South Africa. He might be christened a prominent voice in conflict resolution.

Mohandas Gandhi

Employing nonviolent civil disobedience, Gandhi led India to independence and inspired movements for civil rights and freedom across the world.

Gandhi did not achieve civil right for Indians on a platter of gold. He and the imperial government in South Africa were at odds regarding treatment of Indians in the country. Even in the face of provocation, he remained resolute and focused, applying the *methodology of satyagraha* – devotion to the truth, or non-violent protest. When the oppressive regime pulled the carpet under their feet by enacting an oppressive law against the Indians, Gandhi called on his fellow Indians to defy the new law and suffer the punishments for doing so. Rather than resist through violent means, he urged them to just civilly disobey the law.

He made non-violent resistance his watchword, therefore paving the way for even the most unlikely people to intervene. The harsh methods employed by the South African government in the face of peaceful Indian protesters finally forced South African General Jan Christiaan Smuts (then Minister of Education and colonial secretary in the Transvaal Colony) to negotiate a compromise with Gandhi. While ruling out both verbal and physical violence, he emphasized the principle of Passive Resistance.

His return to his native India did not automatically bring the Indian nation out of the woods. No sooner than he returned to India that he had to face another round of battle with the colonial masters. Carrying the people along, he was able to deal with the British colonial masters in a peaceful manner to achieve independence for India.

Britain granted India its independence on the condition that the once one country would be split into two dominions: India and Pakistan. Gandhi strongly opposed Partition, but he agreed to it in hopes that after independence Hindus and Muslims could achieve peace internally. The idea of partitioning the country precipitated massive riots. Not even Gandhi's encouragement of peaceful coexistence among Hindus and Muslims could dissuade the rioting. He therefore undertook a hunger strike until riots in Calcutta ceased.

One day after he achieved a peaceful resolution of the conflict, Gandhi, on his way to an evening prayer meeting in Delhi on January 30, 1948 was shot to death by a disgruntled Hindu fanatic opposed to Gandhi's efforts to negotiate with Muslims.

Aristotle

Every epoch produces human beings who influence aspects of the people's lives in a given society. Greece at one point was the cradle of human knowledge. Among the intellectuals of the time was Aristotle. He was so intelligent that he was single-handedly picked out to mentor/tutor a thirteen-year old boy who later became Alexander the Great. His knowledge of almost everything the human mind could grasp makes him so outstandingly unique in every sense of the word. He is credited with educating the world. Though originally from Macedonia, Aristotle went to Athens to study under Plato.

When faced with possible execution, his repertoire of intelligence quickly kicked in, propelling him to flee from danger, as opposed to obstinately holding forth and be killed in the process. "Aristotle recalling the fate of Socrates … fled the city, saying that he would not give Athens a chance to sin against philosophy" (Hart, 1992).

Whether his flight was an act of cowardice or really for the reason he gave, he was really prudent. Saddam Hussein of Iraq had a similar premonition, as well as an opportunity to flee but remained obstinate and paid dearly for it. Julius Caesar of the then Roman Empire remained obstinate till death. Col. Muammar el-Qaddafi of Libya stubbornly clung to power, irrespective of all danger signals; he died in the process. The summary is that every great thinker in history at some point escaped danger and still saved both face and life. He knew that it was not time for him to die, Jesus escaped from the Pharisees who plotted to kill him (Mat 12:14-16 NIV).

One prominent postulation of Aristotle was "...the notion that the universe is not controlled by blind chance, by magic, or by the whims of capricious deities, but that its behavior is subject to rational laws..." (Hart). This whole idea of 'nothing in life is left to chance' is what spurs and motivates great innovators and inventors to be creative, irrespective of temporary and ephemeral obstacles. Thomas Aquinas' Five Ways: a proof of the existence of God was in consonance with Aristotelian theory of motion. This aspect of Aristotelian philosophy challenges the evolutionary theory. Aristotle would question the theory that human beings evolved from the apes, as opposed to creation.

Another aspect of Aristotelian postulation worthy of note is the understanding that "Poverty is the parent of revolution and crime...the fate of empires depends on the education of youth" (Hart). Aristotle understands the art of governance: feed the populace, empower the youth and enjoy a peaceful reign. Many a government had fallen because the rulers ignored the Aristotelian principle of leadership. If Karl Marx believed that religion is the opium of the masses, Aristotle affirmed that education of the youth is a means to peaceful governance.

Aristotle lived for only sixty-two years, but his legacy lives on. Although he died in exile, the city of Athens would love to see him return to continue his contributions to human intellectual development. He wrote books ranging from logic to metaphysics, science to the humanities. He was not strictly speaking a theologian, but his theories are the basis for many theological formulations.

If he lived in the modern day Arab region, Aristotle would try to empower the youths of the region, get them busy, educate them, keep them productive so that the Arab Spring would not even flash their occupied and busily productive lives.

Christopher Columbus

Christopher Columbus was born in Italy, in 1451. He later became a ship captain and a navigator. An account has it that his attempt to find a westward route from Europe to the Orient inadvertently discovered the Americas. Columbus' discovery, which inaugurated the age of exploration and colonization in the New World, was one of the critical turning points in history.

Of all the qualities that constituted this great man's popularity, Christopher Columbus' spirit of steadfastness is one capable of spurring anybody into action. His whole mission was a source of encouragement for anyone aspiring to greater heights.

One account had it that in his effort to discover the New World, Christopher Columbus faced a barrage of opposition from members of his own crew. Between September 6 1492 when they left the Canaries and October 12 when they sighted land, the sailors had pressured him to return to Spain, which they left since August 3 because they were frightened and the voyage was getting longer than expected. Because he was determined in his resolve to achieve his goal, he ignored such pressure and discouragement and continued with his journey.

Another aspect of his achievement worthy of note is his discovery opened to the people of Europe two new continents for the settlement of their expanding populations and provides a source of mineral wealth and raw materials that altered the economy of Europe (1992).

When he set out in search of the land, little did Christopher Columbus know that he was going to discover the New World, part of which is the present day continent of North America. Christopher Columbus comes on as a motivator, an achiever, one whose foresight produced one of the greatest continents on earth. His character is a type, which poses a positive influence on the youth and on anyone who intends to make a name for himself and his community.

The down side of Christopher Columbus is that he treated the Indians with shocking cruelty. His discovery was said to have led to the destruction of the civilizations of the American Indians (1992).

Evil is evil anywhere, anytime and in any circumstance. But if Machiavellian dictum: the end justifies the means, is anything to cite, Columbus should not be out rightly condemned. He did what any prince has done and will be willing to do in order to accomplish a mission. Ethically, it is condemnable to destroy another person's heritage in order to build one's empire. This was just what Columbus did for the good of the new world. His statues have been toppled and vandalized in some American cities.

Christopher Columbus represents everyone who aspires to greatness through selfless contributions to human civilization. Although his discovery of the Americas is believed to be accidental, that singular act of courageous voyage later gave rise to the birth of a great nation and the advancement of humanity.

Columbus is featured because, with the turn of world events, he would use his innovation to expand regional boundaries, which would douse most of the tensions relating to territorial disputes around the world. His was also an enviable lifestyle in mediation because he was able to calm frayed nerves of his crew when they felt dampened.

Recent protests against racial inequality and injustice have exposed certain unenviable aspects of the life of Columbus. He is accused of brutalizing Native Americans and plundering their livelihood in his quest for fame. Some even question a popular claim that he discovered the New World. Protesters in major United States cities have defaced, decapitated, touched and toppled Columbus statues.

Charles Schwab

In 1921 Andrew Carnegie picked Charles Schwab to become the first president of the newly formed United States Steel Company. At the age of only thirty-eight, his salary was over one million dollars a year. When asked what qualified him to earn such large salary, he responded: I consider my ability to arouse enthusiasm among my people the greatest asset I possesss, and the way to develop the best that is in a person is by appreciation and encouragement (Carnegie, 1981).

Charles Schwab was knowledgeable enough to be appointed the president of the steel company. However, he became popular not for his expertise in the field of steel production.

He was rather paid highly due to his ability to galvanize his workers' morale and motivate them to fall in love with their work and to feel liked, appreciated and wanted at work. This is a rare charisma, which is needed to douse workplace stress and manage personnel to enhance productivity.

Let it not be a distraction that Schwab's name features in this section. It is strategically placed to demonstrate that even in the midst of chaos, there could be serenity. He was neither a politician nor a warrior. He rather made his mark in the area of organizational prowess. Charles Schwab became a leader simply by worming himself to the hearts of his subjects. Most Arab Spring leaders, to the contrary, forced themselves on the people who endured for as long as the elasticity of their patience lasted.

Robert Mugabe

Mugabe of Zimbabwe does not belong to the list of 100 notable leaders on our purview. As a scholarly work, it is the author's prerogative to discuss him here. He earns a place in this discourse because part of the reason for the Arab Spring was a result of faulty intelligence and dangerous presumptions about the people and their leaders. Zimbabwe came close to suffering a similar fate in the absence of proper awareness.

Although he was not accused of terrorism or terrorism sponsorship, Mugabe earned himself an unenviable title as an enemy of the West. But if all indices were placed right, this needs not be the case.

As far as the story goes, his one crime against the West was his engagement in land redistribution, which did not favor white farmers. The decision might be in bad taste, but what is leadership without taking into consideration the interests of the majority of the population? Again, no leader worth his salt is ever admired by every segment of his constituents.

Every notable leader first looks out for his/her own people before reaching out to the outside world. Posterity might be slow to harshly judge Mugabe if the issue between him and the West is based solely on land redistribution. Zimbabweans, white or black deserve equal ownership of wealth. If Mugabe decided, in his wisdom, to allow every citizen a share in the nation's largesse, so be it.

Although he stubbornly held on to power way into his nineties, his conflict de-escalation was not a total failure. Were it elsewhere that such a military intervention occurred, the conflict would have raged for several years. But in his case, no single gunshot was fired when the military forced him out of office. He died a hero.

Napoleon Bonaparte

Napoleon was a French general and an emperor. He was born in 1769 and graduated from the French military academy in 1785. Napoleon's military exploits started at the age of sixteen. He achieved many successful military expeditions in several foreign countries. However, when he waged war in a failed effort aimed at the invasion of Egypt, his military might was rubbished by the intervention of the British Navy. Napoleon abandoned his army in Egypt and returned to Paris. Napoleon later took over the leadership of France via a coup d' etat. He later edged out his fellow conspirators and became a de facto military dictator.

Napoleon fought and won many foreign wars, but the British military was one formidable force against his invasion and annexation of other countries. When he was restored to power after escaping from Elba, he met his final defeat at Waterloo. After Waterloo, Napoleon was imprisoned by the British on St. Helena, a small island in the south Atlantic (Hart, 1992). He died there in 1821. During the Napoleonic wars, it has been estimated that approximately 500,000 French soldiers died.

However, everything about the dictatorship of Napoleon was not negative. Napoleon was merely an ambitious opportunist, and he had no particular interest in perpetuating horrible massacres. He is credited with selling, in 1803, a vast tract of land to the United States. The Louisiana Purchase, perhaps the largest peaceful transfer of land in all of history, transformed the United States into a nation of near-continental size (1992).

Napoleon is said to have reformed the financial structure and the judiciary. He created the Bank of France and the University of France. He reformed the French civil code. Under the code, there were no privileges of birth.

Augustus Caesar

Augustus Caesar, formerly known as Gaius Octavius, was the grandnephew of Julius Caesar. He was born in 63 B.C. He was an eighteen-year old student when his granduncle, Julius Caesar, then the Roman emperor, was assassinated for intending to end the republican government and install himself a Roman monarch.

Certain conditions were favorable to Augustus Caesar's ascendancy to the Roman power. Julius Caesar, who did not have his own legitimate son, adopted Augustus as his son and in turn had prepared him for a political career. Even when the empire became territorially divided between Augustus and Mark Antony, he skillfully won the support of some of Caesar's legions. Antony who was overly distracted by his romance with Cleopatra lost the war between him and Augustus; as a result, he committed suicide with his sweetheart, thereby becoming the last straw in Augustus' way to power.

The Roman people were obviously frustrated with the trend of events at this point. After many years of civil war and the obvious failure of republican government in Rome, most Romans were willing to accept a benevolent despot, as long as the pretence of democratic rule was continued. Augustus Caesar took advantage of this situation and played on the mentality of the people. Though he had been ruthless during his fight to the top, he was surprisingly conciliatory once he was established in power. It is said that Augustus stands out as perhaps the best example in history of a capable, benevolent despot. He was a true statesman, whose conciliatory policies did much to heal the deep divisions resulting from the Roman civil wars (1992). His conciliatory disposition made him an outstanding mediator of all time.

Napoleon Bonaparte And Augustus Caesar

Napoleon Bonaparte was to France what Augustus Caesar was to Rome. Napoleon was not originally born in France; he was born in Corsica. Augustus Caesar, from every indication, was born into the Roman monarchy, being the grandnephew of Julius Caesar: the great Roman emperor. Both Augustus and Napoleon rose in ranks in the military and political class of Rome and France respectively.

From the foregoing, we see two important personalities who contributed immensely to world history and human advancement. Napoleon is credited with the liquidation of a good number of French soldiers and the oppression of neighbors who refused his advances. Augustus is known to have been so skillful and shrewd in his leadership style. While Napoleon's escapades were international in nature, Augustus was confronted mainly with domestic leadership struggles. Augustus calmed frayed nerves of the Roman people by instituting, in principle, a republican government, for which his uncle, Julius was assassinated. Napoleon busied himself with attacking neighboring states, in an effort to amass territorial and regional vastness. Augustus, on the other hand used every instrument at his disposal to firmly secure his position as the founder of the Roman Empire.

Both men goofed in leadership. Both were brutal, dictatorial, authoritarian and despotic in some ways. But the difference between the two lies in their levels of application. Napoleon applied brute force almost all the way. Augustus applied the wisdom, astuteness and prudence acquired from his uncle, Julius, who prepared him for the challenges of leadership.

Both leaders engaged in some measure of internal brutality on the people they were meant to protect. However, both contributed in no small measure to rewriting world history and (in the case of Napoleon) geography. Napoleon was the one who sold Louisiana to the United States, therefore, making it possible for the United States to gain territorially from Napoleon's recklessness.

If they were contemporaries, the duo would probably have gained a lot from each other. Napoleon would have leant from Augustus how to mix his brutality with some measure of humaneness. As a result, Napoleon would have emulated Augustus' leadership ingenuity and mingled his brutal regime with some measure of reconciliation. While France lost territories during Napoleon's era, Rome prospered under the leadership of Augustus.

Adolf Hitler

History has it that Hitler's rise to power was partly influenced by the Great Depression of 1929. The depression and its aftermaths contributed to Hitler becoming German Chancellor in 1933 at the age of forty-four. Hitler gained the genuine support of most Germans, because he was able to reduce unemployment and generate economic recovery (Hart).

Hitler's German economic prosperity as well as his military dexterity, coupled with the economic woes of superpowers like France and England, drove him to attack and conquer many European nations, including the Soviet Union, which was ruled by another dictator of almost equal trepidation. Hitler's thirst for territorial grabs was not just limited to European nations; the United States had a fair share of his bid to conquer the world. However, Hitler's military valor came crashing after losing his battle for Egypt and Russia. He committed suicide in Berlin in 1945.

In an interview with the SUN newspaper, a former Nigerian finance minister, Olu Falae, recounted a brief history of Hitler's reason for his brutality.

The First World War was a fight over the colonies by the major powers. It ended in 1918 with a treaty, where the allies – British, French, and Americans – defeated Germany and imposed a very one-sided, onerous treaty on Germany, including the payment of reparation by the defeated to the victorious. But the one-sided nature of the treaty enabled Hitler to mobilize the German race and incite them to go into World War II. He told the Germans that Germany has been enslaved. Not only did they lose a war, they are also being made to pay reparation to those who defeated them. That is the hallmark of slavery and Germany must fight to free herself from slavery. The World War II came because of that. More than 70 million people died in that war. But despite that huge loss of lives, it still ended at the negotiating table. We still had Nuremberg to bring that terrible carnage to a close (Saturday, August 13, 2011).

There is no justification for the number of people who died in the hands of Hitler. However, the Western powers cannot, in conscience, completely extricate themselves from complicity in Hitler's evil regime. Hitler's claim that Germany was made to pay reparation after being defeated could not be wished away. It is no news that those conditions that gave rise to Hitler's carnage are still rife in the present world: the rich getting richer at the expense of the less privileged. Hence, the Arab Spring, Black Lives Matter, and the *Occupy* projects had direct bearing on the same conditions that drove Hitler to war.

Joseph Stalin

Stalin is commonly described as one of the dreaded men of his generation. He was of a lowly birth, whose father was a cobbler. He graduated from being an underground Marxist to becoming a prominent member of the Communist Party.

Stalin was known for using and dumping or eliminating his fellow politicians. He formed an alliance with other members of the Politburo, who helped him defeat the left-wing opposition. He later turned against the right wing of the Communist party and defeated them, thereby making himself the sole dictator of the Soviet Union by the early 1930s.

In the course of the years as a ruler, Stalin rounded up opponents and his own partners, forced them to confess to treason and executed them. These purges were extended to both civilians and the armed forces.

Stalin's ruthless use of the secret police and his program of arbitrary arrests and executions and long terms in prison or labor camps for anyone even slightly critical of his rule, succeeded in cowing the population into submission. Stalin's thirst for blood was unleashed even on peasant farmers who resisted his unpopular policy of forced collectivization of agriculture. By Stalin's order, millions of the peasants were either killed or starved to death.

Stalin's hard-heartedness was prominent even with his family members. According to an account, the Germans in World War II captured his only child, Jacob. The Germans offered to exchange him, but Stalin turned the offer down, and Jacob died in a German prison camp (Hart). He was at one point accused of having to do with the death of his second wife after his first died of tuberculosis.

Stalin's USSR conquered and annexed almost all the countries of Eastern Europe. Some put up resistance, while others surrendered without a fight. Latvia, Lithuania and Estonia were among Stalin's easy prey. Poland was shared between Stalin and Hitler.

It is estimated that in the course of his nearly twenty-five years as the ruler of Soviet Union, Stalin sent millions (about 30 million) of persons to their deaths, or to forced labor camps, or had them starved to death.

On the flip side, it is on record that everything about Stalin was not evil and destruction. The rapid industrialization of Soviet Union was attributable to Stalin's administration. Again, during his lifetime, Stalin expanded the borders of the Soviet Union, set up a satellite empire in Eastern Europe, and transformed the USSR into a great power, with influence in every portion of the globe.

Another point worthy of note is that the Cold War was not solely blamed on Stalin. Western leaders had a share in the blame. However, it could be noted that the Cold War era commenced immediately after the World War II as a result of Stalin's expansionist policies and his implacable desire to spread the Communist system—and Soviet power—throughout the world. Joseph Stalin, the seventy-three-year old dictator died in the Kremlin on March 5, 1953.

Adolf Hitler And Joseph Stalin

Adolf Hitler was to Germany what Joseph Stalin was to the Soviet Union. Like Hitler who was originally born in Austria but later became a German, Stalin was born in Georgia, in the

Caucasus and later became the ruler of Soviet Union. Hitler and Stalin impacted world history and peoples' lives in many ways. They brought misery and sent many people to the great beyond. They also contributed to the economic buoyancy of Germany and Soviet Union, and by extension, to the various colonies annexed by the two most dreaded men in history.

Stalin and Hitler were contemporaries as well as partners in crime. They signed a non-aggression pact, but attacked Poland from the west and the east. Between Stalin and Hitler, it is difficult to determine who killed the most people. Both men intimidated and annexed other helpless small countries. Both men contributed a lot in the infrastructure and economic development of their countries and their colonies.

People make excuses for their action or inaction. Hitler and Stalin blamed certain segments of the society for their failure to safeguard the lives of their citizens. Hitler blamed Western powers for his commission of human atrocities. Stalin believed that the Western leaders were to blame for starting the Cold War. At the end of every stalemate between superpowers, the commoners are usually the losers.

If the West and Hitler and Stalin disagreed, none of the tripartite had anything to lose; rather the ordinary citizens lost both lives and property. Hitler took his own life. Stalin died and his body preserved and placed in position of honor at the Red Square. Western powers are still flexing their muscles, intimidating countries, which disagree with them. But the souls of all those who died during the terror years of Stalin and Hitler are not resting in peace until there is justice in the world. It was the quest for peace and egalitarianism, in the first place that gave rise to virtually all the agitations spreading all over the globe.

Leadership Styles

Politics and leadership have been implicated in crises in human circles. That being the case, it becomes worthwhile to discuss some notable *Leadership styles*. In this regard, therefore, three leadership styles come into focus. But *Participative Leadership* takes the front burner. This does not in any way make participative leadership the best style. It is rather based on the fact that participative leadership seems to be the norm all over the world. It is not perfect, but compared to authocratic and delegative leadership styles, participative leadership is more widespread and tends to involve a larger representation of the populace.

Although the terms 'participative' and 'democratic' seem synonymous in principle, they are worlds apart in practice. The reason they are far apart is that many democratic systems are only democratic in name; every other aspect is either authoritarian or delegative. In the former, leaders make decisions independently with little or no input from the rest of the group. In the latter, leaders offer little or no guidance to group members and leave decision-making up to group members. While these are two extremes, participative lies in the middle.

In the participative leadership style, also known as the democratic leadership, leaders offer guidance to group members, but they also participate in the group and allow input from other group members (Cherry, 2011). Participative leaders encourage group members to participate, but retain the final say over the decision-making process. Group members feel engaged in the process and are more motivated and creative. This is what makes the leadership style of democracy so proactive, because the leader is involved in almost every single aspect of governance. The leader may not be directly involved, but is always at alert, to break the tie in the event of a deadlock.

The three arms might seem to operate independently, but in the end, the chief executive is the overall charge. There are, however, strict exceptions to the process. Though in charge, the chief executive carefully observes the rule of checks-and-balances. Otherwise, any apparent arbitrariness might result in an impeachment.

Although the participative style of leadership has all these lofty angles, it is also fraught with challenges. The authocratic leader gets things done and done fast, even if the people may not be happy about it. The delegative leader is seen as nonchalant and lackluster; at least, the people are happy that they are delegated to run the affairs of the government. But in participative leadership, simple matters are overheated because everyone's opinion is considered.

A good example is the government of the United States which runs a participative style of leadership. In an effort to have everyone on board, it wastes a lot of time argueing and debating over issues, sometimes, to the detriment of the common good. A clear case is the Debt Ceiling debate by the United States congress. The debate raged on for weeks, and was eventually agreed upon on the eve of the deadline. The casualty was the credit rating that was downgraded from tripple A to bouble A+.

Plato had some reservation for democratic government after the government of Athens executed Socrates. It was not only Socrates who suffered at the altar of participative government. Mannuel Noriega, Saddam Hussein, Robert Mugabe, et al, have either been eliminated, imprisoned or hated in the name of promoting the participative ideals.

Nonetheless, irrespective of all of its negetive aspects, participative is still considered the best of the three leadership styles because the interest of the majority is represented, or seems to be represented.

Leadership is a charism, which is not possessed by just any human being. Some are born into royalty, others acquire leadership skills. William and Harry, for instance, were not the only male children born in Britain, yet they automatically became princes by the simple reason that they were born the same year their mates were born, the only difference being that their parents are from the royal family.

Some people are better followers; they just are not disposed to the rigors of leadership. For such people, their interest is either not into leadership or they are apartheic to leaders and resentful of the positions leaders occupy. History has shown that a society without a leader is a failed society. Somalia, for many years, was without a central leadership. This could lead to anarchy, and it did in Somalia when various factions were terrorizing people and taking hostage of citizens and tourists on land and on high seas. It has happened in many other societies across the globe. Those nations with a functional government still grapple with serious security challenges; imagine a nation without a central authority.

It is considered a patriotic duty for one to volunteer or be appointed or elected to lead. Imposition of a leader is not only immoral and unethical; it is an insult on the people's intelligence and, therefore, a quick way to commit political suicide. Most Arab countries and beyond have witnessed rulers staying in power till death did them part. So the Arab Spring was a way to remind other long term rulers to be prudent and leave when the ovation is loudest. Mali's President Ibrahim Boubacar Keita and Sudan's President Omar al-Bashir probably learnt in a hard way that when the same people who placed them in power rose up against them, they had no choice but to abdicate.

X

MEDIATION AND CULTURAL TYPES

Personality traits, cultural differences, environmental influences, temperaments, and a host of other conditions are among the factors influencing dialogue and mediation, especially in the culturally diverse and conflict-ridden regions of the globe.

One way of understanding the recurrent conflicts, which finally gave rise to the Arab Spring and other forms of conflicts around the world, is to examine the various cultural forms. It is also this diversity in cultures that seems to be the bane of a lasting peace in the world. While one region employs a certain approach to a problem, the other wants it another way; both justifiably rationalizing their approach and holding on to their position. Further discussion of some of the various cultures might help to better understand them.

Western

Pragmatism is the predominant characteristic of American business culture. Potential for profitability nurtures business relationships, and trust is often found in the terms of a binding contract. Trust, or lack thereof, profoundly influences American negotiation practices. American businesspersons prefer a straightforward dialog where needs and concerns are addressed somewhat candidly. Through a position of strength and openness each side works to make concessions until a mutually beneficial agreement can be reached. This willingness to make concessions is motivated by pragmatism—the willingness to avoid unnecessary time and expense (Sgubini, Norman).

South & Central American

Brazilians are known for being warm and friendly people in personal life and in business relations. This attitude is pleasant and welcoming. However, it may create an informal mediation environment that may not please mediators from other cultures. Many business people characterize the way Brazilians do business as somewhat informal. Nonetheless, some other values come in place when they are negotiating. Regarding these values, Brazilians ranked honesty, trustworthiness and ethics as being essential during the negotiation process. Transparency and punctuality are also important factors in order to show a party is acting in good faith and is trustworthy. Finally, it is important to build a business relationship before starting mediation, this way the parties will try to communicate to each other the image of an honest, trustworthy and ethical person, able to duly carry on a successful mediation (Potenza, Sgubini).

Central European

Credibility and social reputation when dealing with Italian businesses are decisive factors for successful mediation. Generally, business people in Italy prefer to negotiate and maintain a business relationship with an executive or manager of a firm. Elegance and appearance are important considerations in Italian culture. More so than in many other countries an attractive, well-dressed individual is considered more reliable. Italians prefer to take their time negotiating and be familiar with who they're talking to. Indeed, being in a rush to sign an agreement will lead to unfulfilled expectations. For example, during a business lunch it is important to begin with relaxed conversation; giving your partner the opportunity of enjoying lunch before you get to the subject you're interested in (Sgubini, Cardinale).

Eastern European

Negotiations with Russians often involve flared tempers. During negotiations and meetings, temper tantrums and walkouts often occur. As a foreigner, you are expected to be on time to all business appointments. However, your Russian counterpart may be late, as this may be a test of your patience. Do not expect an apology from a late Russian, and do not demonstrate any kind of attitude if your business appointments begin one or two hours late. This may also be a test of your patience. Do not show the soles of your shoes, as this is considered impolite. They are considered dirty, and should never come in contact with any type of seat. Be alert and open to taking a drink or having a toast, as refusing to do so is a serious breach of etiquette. Speaking or laughing loudly in public is considered rude, as Russians are generally reserved and somber (Hofstede, Priest).

Middle Eastern

Religion plays a very important role in most of the countries of the Middle East. The predominant religion for the Arab and Middle Eastern countries is Islam. Muslims follow the doctrines of the Koran. The entire lifestyle of the middle easterners is highly influenced by their religion. They have no clear demarcation between religious and civil responsibilities. Sometimes, the roles of their religious leaders are interwoven with their religious duties. This is an important piece of information, which a mediator to the region must know.

African

Africa is a diverse continent, comprising various ethnic groups with their own cultures and idiosyncrasies. It, therefore, becomes difficult to typify the continent. However, apart from Egypt, which has been characterized the cradle of civilization, some segments of Ethiopian culture have ancient cultural heritage that may be representative of African people. Though their life is hard, the Amhara of Ethiopia are a proud people, proud of their ethnicity, religion and their special place in the world. Their culture is strong, developed over many centuries, and it has withstood the incursions of outside governments and religions (Bender, 1971).

From this quotation, it is understood that the Amharas can do all it takes to protect their pride. A mediator who is not originally from the region must be acquainted with the sensitivity of the people and treat them accordingly. Their strong character manifests in all aspects of their life including in interpersonal disputes.

Asian

Asians place a great deal of importance on relationships. The building of long lasting relationships is tantamount for business success in Asia. The concept of "saving face" is inherent in this region. Asians will go to great lengths to save face and avoid embarrassment. The loss of face is not easily forgotten nor is it easily forgiven. Do not use large hand movements. The Chinese do not speak with their hands. Your movements may be distracting to your host. Do not point when speaking. Bowing or nodding is the common greeting; however, you may be offered a handshake. Wait for the Chinese to offer their hand first. Allow the Chinese to leave a meeting first (Hofstede, Priest).

These are facts, which can aid a mediator from another cultural region to have a successful session in the Asian culture.

Mediation Types And Specific Cultures

Cultural Type:	Challenge to Mediation:	Mediation Type that May Work Best:
Western (Christianity)	Presumed Pragmatism – Mediation could be stalled when it is assumed that each session must produce a quick result.	Workplace Mediation
South & Central American (Christianity)	Informal Negotiating Environment - Mediation is a serious business, which certainly demands a serious setting. This culture seems to over-simplify mediation.	Interpersonal Mediation

Central European (Christianity)	Preference to negotiate with an executive over a delegate - In this regard, mediation could suffer a serious setback in the absence of an authority figure as opposed to an intelligent mediator who is not an executive.	Landlord / Tenant Mediation
Eastern European (Orthodox)	Temper tantrums - Tantrums are bound to flare up in negotiations, but incessant temper tantrums could hinder mediation.	School or family Mediation
Middle Eastern (Islam)	Religious inclination – It is believed that everything in Islamic culture is governed by religion. Since different interest groups could engage in mediation, would they be accommodated?	Nonprofit Organizations and Community-based Mediation
African (Animism)	Over Protection of cultural identity – Cultural identity is the pride of a people. But in mediation, the disputants might focus on culture, to the detriment of the main cause of crisis, thereby defeating the purpose of mediation.	Environmental and property ownership Mediation
Asian (Buddhism)	No use of hand gestures – For a mediator coming from the West, this could be a challenge, in the sense that most westerners buttress points by hand gesticulations.	Discrimination and racially charged Mediation

XI

CONFLICT RESOLUTION VERSUS PROPAGANDA

The press community as the fourth estate of government is as important as the government of the day. This means that the entire populace looks up to the media for not just information on government activities, also for entertainment and unbiased situation reporting of events around the globe.

In the United States, for instance, some historical antecedents point to the fact that this whole idea of a press secretary is not as old as the United States government. "It was not until after President Abraham Lincoln's administration that Congress formally appropriated funds for a White House Staff, which at first consisted merely of a Secretary" (Dale, 1998).

Since the Press Department has come to be an integral part of the government, paid for by the American people, it is only expedient that the people expect the department to do a satisfactory and worthwhile job of information dissemination. But just as every other aspect of a democratic system, the press has, for the most part, been highly politicized.

Instead of political bickering and viewpoints, the press could devote time to enlighten the public regarding government's important decisions and policies as they affect the ordinary citizenry. This becomes necessary as Dr. Kendall Hope rightly observes:

> The time spent expressing partisan views is wasted time that could be spent educating our American public about many objective pieces of information that ... include a better past and present coverage of the Iraqi culture and people (2008).

Taking a cue from the American press, it is public that the various media houses have their own political biases and favorites. However, these partisan interests should be kept out of the press briefings by the chief press secretary of White House. One way of keeping to the business of the day at such briefings is for the editors of these media houses to remind their reporters that press briefings are different from political meetings. The reporters should come to the briefing with a mind set at the subject of the day and try to avoid questions, which clearly detract from the issue at stake.

Having said this, the blame does not lie squarely with the media houses. The White House Press department should focus on issues aimed at just communicating the workings of the government, as opposed to comparing the present administration with any other administration. It is also not a forum for bolstering the ego of the president or of the ruling party. It must not be a forum to vilify other party interests and figures. Even in the event of out-of-context questions, the press secretary should show professionalism and control the flow in order to reduce or prevent frequent political vitriol associated with some media outfits.

The Press Secretary can use the press briefings to inform the American people of the need to engage in those overseas operations that cost them so much human and material resources. It could be an opportunity to address steps taken by the government to bolster the image of America adversely influenced by what some might term unjust operations, influences and interferences in internal affairs in the Middle East. It could also be an opportunity to reach out to the representatives of the Middle East countries in conflict to let them understand that America is not an occupying force. They should be made to understand the mission of America to these countries - mediation mission: mission that must be accomplished for peace to reign.

"Truth can be established through good investigative journalism and in-depth educational study and programming" (Hope). Investigative journalism is an aspect, which has suffered neglect in some media houses. Some news networks are so sensationalized that one begins to wonder what the future holds for journalism.

Many American news networks have won large number of admirers. In the same vein, these same networks are losing objective admirers through unbalanced and unfair news reporting. As influential broadcast and print media, these organizations engaged objective writers, broadcasters, and contributors whose personal and collective views used to be all-inclusive. But the dynamics gradually changed from popular programming to partisan bickering. It is only a few of these networks that are somewhat subtle and sensitive.

If the media outlets should employ the same intensity with which they bicker in the dissemination of the truth of the Middle East conflicts, the outcome of the conflicts might be different. The news media can take some time to express solidarity with families of veteran military men and women in conflict-ridden areas of the Middle East. The media can educate the Arab region regarding their relationship with the West. They can use their rich programming and wide audience to reach areas of the world that are ignorant of the main cause of tensions in the Middle East and to reassure the people of the region that a few bad elements in their society should not be a source of consternation between the West and the Arabs.

If propaganda is akin to the use of information to sway public opinion toward one person's or group's views, it could be correct to conclude that the use of propaganda is immoral, unethical, unorthodox, irresponsible and an expression of desperation and, to an extent, helplessness. It could be related to the proverbial drowning person reaching out to grab anything in his/her way to remain afloat.

Conflicts often reach fever pitch by the activities of propagandists. Insurgents use propaganda to either justify their cause or to advance their violent interests. For instance, during the uprising between the Egyptian government and the Muslim Brotherhood over the former President Morsi's detention, it was alleged that members of the Brotherhood inflated figures and made up stories to curry public sympathy. One such case was the use of fire extinguisher by the Brotherhood inside the mosque to paint a picture of government forces tear-gassing them.

To maintain a leading role in mediation efforts, especially in the Middle East, the American Government press department, State Department and indeed American media outlets should have a leading role of either countering negative propaganda or correcting erroneous impressions by rebel and terrorist groups. This should be the most powerful tool to de-escalate conflicts all over the peace-loving world.

XII

PROSPECTS OF CONFLICT RESOLUTION AND DE-ESCALATION

An actual session of Alternative Dispute Resolution (ADR) enlightenment with young people in South Dakota.

According to the Holy Books,

There is a time for everything, and a season for every activity under the heavens:

- a time to be born and a time to die, a time to plant and a time to uproot
- a time to kill and a time to heal, a time to tear down and a time to build
- a time to weep and a time to laugh, a time to mourn and a time to dance
- a time to scatter stones and a time to gather them, a time to embrace and a time to refrain from embracing
- a time to search and a time to give up, a time to keep and a time to throw away
- a time to tear and a time to mend, a time to be silent and a time to speak
- a time to love and a time to hate, a time for war and a time for peace (Ecclesiastes 3:1-8 *New International Version (NIV)*.

This quote seems to sum up the mission of conflict de-escalation and mediation efforts anywhere in the human family. At one point in history, the Middle Eastern region was classified the cradle of civilization. What this means is that the present day so-called super powers and first worlds copied or emerged from the region. Nonetheless, as generations progressed, the region gradually slid into a harbinger of violence, religious plurality and all sorts of anti civilizing activities, including in recent years, modern warfare involving the gulf war. It seems the gulf war had the most devastating effect in the lives and well being of the people of the once historically progressive and culturally endowed region. As the region that produced notable historic figures – including Jesus Christ and Prophet Mohammed, one would expect that the region would be as peaceful as paradise. This expectation seems a far cry.

The aftermaths of major conflicts of the magnitude of war are destruction, human impoverishment, and guilt. Restitution often follows such devastation. However, rebuilding infrastructures may be achieved within a timeframe and with good budgeting. But to rebuild devastated humanity is a huge project, which may never be achieved. For the sake of argument, it begs the question to say that human life is never ever revamped. History has it that several centuries ago, a certain Jewish-born individual was cruelly murdered. This individual, through some mysterious powers, came back to life after three days. Before and after this event, the only one who has risen from the dead is Jesus Christ. Every other dead is dead for good. Even when individuals claim to rise from the dead, usually for medical reasons, they hardly live long thereafter.

So, it behooves only American magicians to tell the world how best to resurrect all the innocent men, women, children and ordinary Iraqis killed in that senseless war. It is such a sad reality, which makes peace-loving people feel sick to their heart with every passing day that such experience continues – all of the violence in the Middle East specifically – because it is truly a unique geographic and cultural microcosm of violence" (Hope).

In rebuilding the Middle East, the international community in collaboration with Arab leaders should first employ the services of professional mediators to calm frayed nerves in the region. This becomes necessary because it could be an exercise in futility to build the bricks without first building the body and mind of the intended brick dweller.

In this context, therefore, the role of the professional mediators would be to get the various interest and splinter groups to present their grievances with a view to discussing them at the highest places. This will also be an opportunity for the coalition forces to admit their mistakes and be humble about it. This is one cardinal principal of a peaceful mediation. "One of our basics of fair and respectful interactions from one person or group of people to another is acknowledging when one or a group has done something wrong and very sincerely apologizing for it" (2008).

As part of the rebuilding project, the coordinators must engage the services of professional counselors and mediators. Their role would be to reach out to the warring factions and their leadership and to get them understand that there is more to life than just incessant warfare. Since it is not possible to round off all the militia to counsel them, a national reorientation project would surely work. This would serve as a teachable moment for citizens who might be nursing the idea of negative indoctrination, which is the bane of peace and security. "To not provide them education about the American people will allow the same forces within the Iraqi culture who are educating them falsely, to continue to indoctrinate them falsely about our intentions" (2008).

It is only when individuals are appropriately conscientized to respect life and property that any meaningful infrastructure rebuilding and lasting peace will succeed. To talk of peace, justice must be present; otherwise, it becomes a charade, a mere exercise in futility and a clear possible obstacle to progress.

Incessant wars and other forms of violence have not helped peace efforts in the Middle East. Assassinations of notable personalities of the region remain a big obstacle towards the attainment of lasting peace in the area. For instance, the entire invasion of Iraq might seem a defeat of a despot; it should also be known as a regrettable mistake. The most tragic aspect of that invasion was the culmination to the hanging of Saddam Hussein. Until this generation of Iraqis passes, the mark left by his death remains indelible. He had loyalists and relatives who felt betrayed by other segments of Iraqis. He had soldiers and other security experts who were happier under his regime. These people might want to avenge the death of their mentor and hero in any way, shape or form. The same Iraq mistake was later repeated in Libya. Since Muammar al-Gaddafi was killed, Libya has not, and may never be the same again.

Lack of trust is another reason why it is difficult to accomplish any meaningful rebuilding of relationships in the Arab region. An average Arab citizen views Western activities with suspicion. In the same vein, the West approaches the Arab with a good amount of caution. Arabs believe that the West is out to pillory their rich cultural heritage and plunder their natural resources. Some people in the West see most Arabs as out to harm every westerner in their view. Insofar as there is mutual distrust among the groups, any meaningful relationship rebuilding is a far cry and difficult to attain.

Economic factors pose yet another major obstacle to rebuilding of relationships in the region since the world economy plummets in recent years. To start a reasonable rebuilding of relationships, words of mouth are not just enough. The international community can extend a hand of friendship to the people of the region by engaging in several works of charity to the people who have been impoverished by wars and violence. If already committed funds were reallocated from military operations to a better representation of ambassadors or emissaries, this would begin a path toward a better use of the investment of U.S. money and energy.

Politics is one issue, which may not be easily wished away in an effort to rebuild relationships in the region. Each successive government has its own agenda and areas of interest. It is the Democrats today; it might be the Republicans tomorrow. Each of the parties has various policies regarding how to deal with issues of foreign relations.

It is being suggested that the onus of *conscience* is on the United States and the allied forces to rebuild Iraq as much as possible without any conditions and strings because they took their war to Iraq. Iraq did not wage war against any of the allied nations. Since the war was not justified in the first place, America and the other involved nations owe it to the people of Iraq to return their country to the same shape they found it. This might be a herculean task, which may not be attainable. But it does not hurt to try, for the sake of justice and fairness.

It could be tough, but not impossible to:

- begin to understand cultural and sub-cultural differences
- implement needs for respect
- utilize language and culture to foster peace.

These are truly reachable goals if those in power will simply embrace the validity of conflict resolution and education in cultural interactions and respect for people. If implemented with patience and caring, it would be amazing how much things could change toward peace in time.

Vestiges of conflicts and Glimmer of Hope

Most fairy tales end with: *They lived happy ever after.* However, war tones are different. Peace lovers likely wish war stories could be told with the same or similar gusto. Wars and their attendant devastation never end happily, irrespective of victor or vanquished. The victors, even when they gloat in their gallantry, live with guilt ever after. As for the vanquished, they wallow in regrets, shame, and humiliation all the days of their life.

A glaring example is the declaration of *No Victor, No Vanquished* at the end of the Nigeria-Biafra civil war by the then Head of state, General Yakubu Gowon. Laudable and conciliatory this declaration may sound, the reality on ground does not buttress the statement. The war ended in favor of Nigerian government, which dictates the pace of things. It decides the trajectory of events for both winners and losers of the civil conflict. It dictates whether or not to claim victory. The Biafran side had to live with the humiliation and deprivation for as long as the victorious Nigerian side is willing to integrate it into the affairs of the rest of the nation.

This situation is almost similar to relationships between Western powers and the Arab world. Although reeling from the vestiges of incessant conflicts, on a note of optimism, a peaceful Middle East would be so nice that the region could compete with the rest of the prosperous countries in terms of economic and sociological prosperity.

Apart from competing with other developed worlds in economic and sociological prosperity, a peaceful Middle East would certainly focus on returning to its historic glorious days, when the world recognized the region as a cradle of civilization. This recognition would in turn bolster the tourism potentials of the Persian Gulf states.

A peaceful Middle East would focus more on religious liberalization, in which individuals would be free to worship their God according to the dictates of their conscience and choosing, rather than one based on family and tribal tradition of one religion for all.

A peaceful Middle East would educate its citizens, and by so doing defeat superstition, which has been the bane of progress and development in the region.

As a region surrounded by arid deserts, artificial boundaries may not be easily delineated. However, there are ethnic and religious boundaries, which could form natural borders. For instance, all language, ethnic and religious groupings could have their different nation states. When the nations speak one language, understand each other's cultural sensitivities, they tend to live in peace with each other.

Many an optimist believes there is hope for a lasting peace in the volatile Middle East. The best approach to this lasting peace is the engagement of proactive and seasoned mediators.

Judging by the ethnic and cultural tensions and diversity amongst the dwellers of the Middle East, representative democratic form of government would be ideal for the region.

Representative democracy is a form of democracy in which citizens allow others — usually elected officials — to represent them in government processes and are not necessarily directly involved in any of the processes of legislation or lawmaking (Conjecture Corporation, 2003 – 2012). However, if representative democracy sounds western, Middle Easterners may formulate their own version of it. They need to create their own name for it – to own it – to make it their own satisfies an important need in this region. When they "own" their own solution and it is not given or forced on them, they will work to keep it. This seems a central point for a workable option toward peace for the Middle East. It must be religious liberation (biased term) but defined in their own terms and specifics in every way and be incorporated into their governmental structure as well.

Some of the nations of the region base their governments on the monarchical or theocratic systems. Even when they have a representative structure or the democratic constitution, some still base their government on family succession. For instance, Syrian president, Bashar Hafez al-Assad, succeeded his father who was the former president. He is believed to achieve this feat due to his father's position. An account had it that the Syrian Parliament unanimously approved the nomination of the late President Hafiz al-Assad's son, Dr. Bashar al-Assad to become the 16th President of the Syrian Arab Republic" (café-Syria.com, 2012). There have been a few other places where similar approvals have been made due to circumstances of the moment: North Korea's Kim Jong-un; Congo DRC's Joseph Kabila; Togo's Faure Gnassingbé Eyadéma.

It was also strongly believed that Saddam Hussein of Iraq was grooming one of his sons to succeed him. That chapter ended with the coalition invasion and subsequent liquidation of the president and his two sons.

In Iran, for instance, at the top of Iran's power structure is the Supreme Leader, Ayatollah Ali Khamenei, who succeeded Ayatollah Rouhollah Khomeini, the father of the Iranian Revolution (*Iran Chamber Society*, 2012).

Other strategies of conflict de-escalation are as suggested: The Kurds in Iraq and Kuwait could combine to ask for nationhood, if that is a panacea for peaceful coexistence in the region. Same goes for the Arabs in both countries.

If the people of the region would be happier splintering into religious groups, the Shiites are large enough to form a government. The Sunnis are equally large to seek statehood. These groups can appoint, elect or select their own people to represent and govern them.

The West, therefore, has no business meddling in the affairs of a people who have internally decided on what structure of government that is workable for them. If the region were left alone to manage their own affairs, there would be relative peace and tranquility in the region and the world as a whole. External interference could justifiably be blamed for instability in the region. "We continue to try and make them play by our rules, and lives continue to be lost while we spin our wheels doing this" (Hope, 2008).

Identifying With the Locals

As part of de-escalation strategy in already tense regions of the world, it is pertinent to note and avoid triggers of further tension. To further explicate this point, an analogy becomes relevant here. A certain healthcare worker recounts: In the course of my outpatient nursing clinics, I have encountered adults who would almost cry at the sight of me wearing a lab coat. If they get through that first stage of fear and anxiety, they usually turn around and exhale with a sense of relief that the procedure was not as bad as expected. It is not usually my presence that creates the anxiety; it is the fact that my lab coat reminds them of their childhood experience whereby their parents took them to a doctor wearing a lab coat, holding a needle, which inflicted pain.

"For the people of Iraq, the mere sight of a uniform stimulates many more feelings of terror and expectation than Americans can begin to imagine" (Hope). In this regard, therefore, a proper approach would be to prioritize operations according to need – probably dependent on volatility or otherwise of any given location. What this means is that civilian aid workers whose mission is non-combatant should cover areas where locals need food, water and medicine. For the most part, insurgents very rarely target charity workers, whether they are soldiers or civilians insofar as they are dressed like everyone around – not military uniform, though.

As for soldiers who battle terrorists on daily basis, wearing of uniform may not only help them to execute their mission properly, it would also enable them to recognize each other as soldiers, different from militants.

When it comes to the emissaries and diplomats to the region, they should identify with the culture of the people and dress appropriately. For instance, if a female Secretary of States were to meet with the Emir of Baghdad, though American and representing American interest, dressing like an average Iraqi woman for just that purpose would not make her less of a Secretary or American.

Dressing like the people is a way of identifying with them. By identifying with them, there is less tension and suspicion by the people. This is where relationships begin to heal, and the people begin to develop trust in the American mission in the region.

CONCLUSION

Algeria, Bahrain, Comoros, Djibouti, Egypt, Iran, Iraq, Israel, Jordan, Kuwait, Lebanon, Libya, Mauritania, Morocco, Oman, Palestinian Territories, Qatar, Saudi Arabia, Somalia, Sudan, Syria, Tunisia, United Arab Emirates, Yemen are the countries located within a geographical and cultural zone known as the Arab world, mainly in the Middle East. While peace and stability have become a rare commodity allover the world, some of the countries mentioned here seem to have a fair share of restiveness.

It sounds like an irony of life that God's own land, of all places on earth, refuses to know peace irrespective of numerous efforts at peaceful resolution and de-escalation of conflicts in the Middle East. As the region that produced notable historic figures – including Jesus Christ and Prophet Mohammed, one would expect that the region would be so peaceful and habitable. So far, the opposite seems to be the case.

Scholars and common-interest individuals arguably believe a curse was brought upon the region by their ancestors. They relate it to activities surrounding the unjust crucifixion of one of their sons. It should be recalled that after Pontius Pilate washed his hands clean of any complicity in the death of Jesus

Christ, the Jews did not mince words to declare, "Let his blood be on us and our children" (Matt. 27:25). Jews are not, strictly speaking, Arabs; however, territorially, they mingle with Arabs and occupy a geographical region, which they share in common.

Some of the salient issues discussed in this work are recurrent and controversial in nature. They recur in the sense that peace talks have been ongoing and broken for years on end. The topics are controversial because Western involvement, which was originally designed to be a solution, has not really attained that purpose. Some of those aspects worthy of note are as itemized and discussed herein.

Prior to the advent of the Arab Spring, the Middle East had known and endured rulers who ruled the people in the same fashion as the ancient Pharaohs. One of those modern day pharaohs was Saddam Hussein, whose government was somewhat ruthless. He flaunted his wealth and demonstrated that power rested in him and his cohorts. Like everything, which had a beginning and an end, Saddam rose, reigned and fell, thanks to the United States forces. While many applauded his fall, the manner of that fall leaves an indelible and regrettable mark in the land of the ancient Mesopothemia till date. Saddam and his sons were killed, a situation, which further fueled the simmering conflicts even beyond Iraq. That was a case of mediation gone wrong.

Seasoned mediators would have handled the Iraq conflict differently. The United States government and its allies should have focused more on building a bridge to let Saddam give up some or all of his political powers, while wielding the option of war as the Best Alternative To a Negotiated Agreement (BATNA).

Best Alternative To a Negotiated Agreement refers to the course of action that will be taken by a party engaged in negotiations if the talks fail and no agreement can be reached. Having a good BATNA can help you negotiate on the merits. Rather than stubbornly clinging to one's position, a good mediator, equipped with a powerful BATNA recognizes when to make compromises in order to arrive at a negotiated and binding agreement. One who has a better and stronger BATNA usually presents the matter and discusses it according to its own merit. This principle saves both time and effort, and gives rise to a much-needed agreement. Developing a good BATNA not only enables one to determine what is a minimally acceptable agreement, it will probably raise the minimum (Ury, 1991).

At no epoch has war been of any benefit to anyone. The government, soldiers, and the civil populace have a lot to lose in a war situation. For instance, after the war in Iraq, the devastation was so enormous that the United States and the Iraqi government joined forces to rebuild the once beautiful city of Baghdad and for the most part, other cities in Iraq. They may rebuild the infrastructure as much as possible, but the human toll can never be the same again.

In this light, therefore, the United States government can save face by looking for a way to get the Arab world understand that the crisis in the Middle East is not a show of Western military might rather than a service to an oppressed populace. This can be achieved by empowering the locals to confront their own issues by talking with the various interest groups with a view to address their own concerns and grievances and to formulate their own mutual agreement.

By so doing, western countries can demonstrate a good measure of transparency in mediating in conflicts in the Middle East. This will go a long way in correcting the notion that seems to suggest that Western intervention in the region was aimed at protecting western interests. For instance, it was widely believed that the United States took the war to the Persian Gulf in order to deal with the terrorists over there and protect lives and property in the United States. Laudable as the policy might sound, the ideal thing would have been to formulate strategies in Iraq toward goals that will serve the needs of the Iraqi people, instead of *our interpretation* of what they need..." (Hope: 2008).

The situation that gave rise to the Arab Spring did not just happen in one day; it was a series of events perpetrated by the same set of rulers who lorded it over the people for as long as it lasted. When the people spoke in one voice, they confronted the status quo. The resultant effect was the dismantling of governments, which were hitherto untouchable. That was a lesson in governance, which sent shivers to the entire Arab region and the rest of the world. Perpetuity in government as well as taking the citizenry for granted was checkmated. The Arab Spring protesters reclaimed freedom of expression and of association.

Mediation is a serious business as well as a sensitive one. Therefore, if the setting is wrongly chosen and or arranged, the outcome might be counter-productive. The Arab Spring and its attendant transition bottleneck could have been averted if mediators took thorough consideration of the vastness and the diverse nature of the Arab region. The physical setting could have an impact on facilitating communication, gaining control of the argument, reducing or increasing pressure on the parties, and insuring the safety of all those involved (Chan, Leviton, Greenstone).

Neutrality of venue and mediators cannot be overemphasized for the success of mediation in general. Privacy, security, accessibility are some of the factors to consider in mediation. It is also important that the disputants must feel equally empowered. Power imbalance can ruin a well-planned mediation session.

The general rule for mediation setting, whether in the Arab world or in interpersonal disputes, include the following:

- Everyone should be able to see and hear everyone else and participate easily in discussions.
- Members of one party should be able to sit together if they choose. Couples typically want to sit side by side.
- Everyone should be physically comfortable, undistracted, and feel as safe as possible.
- The mediators should be able to control the process.
- The setting should suggest mediator impartiality.
- Pick a location that feels comfortable and private: not too large, not too dim or cluttered.
- The suitable furniture for mediation is a round table or a square table, or a rectangular table. The sitting arrangement is strictly important (Beer, Steief).

A conflict, which was as convoluted as the Arab Spring would require seasoned and experienced mediators who possess certain natural qualities not taught or learned in school.

Appropriate mediators should possess intelligence, tact, drafting skills, a sense of humor, and have specific knowledge and expertise of the conflict at hand. Mediators who possess these attributes are likely to be acceptable to all sides in a conflict, and consequently enhance the parties' motivation to reach a peaceful settlement (Bercovitch).

Conflict resolution cuts across various spectra of life. Therefore, for the mediator, whether he or she is religious or animist is irrelevant. Whether he is black or white has no place. Nonetheless, certain qualities remain non-negotiable. Apart from being and remaining neutral, he or she must be talented. The talent is reflected in the sensitivity with which the mediator listens, hears, responds, empathizes, creates, draws parties into the process and deftly maneuvers through the delicate and difficult moments with an intuitive sense of timing and appropriateness.

The following qualities are also expected of any dedicated mediator: Process facilitator, discussion facilitator, clarifier, idea generator, face-saver, agent of reality, messenger, distinguisher of needs from wants, and trainer (Chan, Leviton, Greenstone).

Mediation requires tact and orderliness. Therefore, these four stages of mediation must be followed.

Stage 1: Opening Statement

The mediator discusses the process, and describes the mediator's role, the roles of the participants, and the general expectations for the mediation session. The purposes of the Opening Statement include the following:

- establish a safe environment to negotiate
- establish the mediator's credibility and control of the proceedings
- explain the mediation process and what will be asked of the parties
- obtain necessary commitments from the parties concerning their involvement
- be sensitive to concerns raised by the parties.

Before the actual commencement of mediation, the mediator must assure the disputants of his/her neutrality. The disputants must make a commitment to respect each other's time and values. Expectations are also pointed out to the parties in regard to their commitment to the time required for resolving the issues, after which they are requested to provide their consent to commence the process (Chan).

Stage 2: Information Sharing and Issue Identification

- Ask each disputant to state their perception of the conflict. Hear all evidence pertinent to the dispute. Collect any evidence relating to the dispute, such as written contracts, cancelled checks, receipts, and reports.
- Clarify issues.
- Clarify remaining differences and see whether the disputants can form a common understanding.
- Listen actively to the disputants' issues and feelings as they are talking:
- Learn about the parties' interests and priorities.
- Determine whether the parties agree on the credibility of the incidents and information.

- Clarify the differences and see whether the parties can form a common understanding.
- Formulate clear goals.
- Attempt to settle simple issues. Build on success.
- Note parties' underlying needs and hopes. These are at the core of the dispute. Having them addressed and met will be the core of a resolution. (Chan, Leviton Greenstone).

Stage 3: Exchange and Negotiation.

This stage encompasses problem solving, but not limited to it. At this stage, parties

- identify and evaluate a range of ideas
- negotiate with everyone's interests in mind
- develop and test specific proposals
- gain confidence in their ability to resolve the situation and to build commitment to the emerging agreement (Chan, Beer, Stief).

Stage 4: Agreement and Conclusion

The following are the elements that an agreement should contain.

- Details specifics: who, what, when.
- Is evenhanded and not conditional
- Uses clear, familiar wording
- Emphasizes positive action
- Deals with any pending proceedings
- Provides for the future (Chan, Beer, Stief).

It is not just sufficient to apply the above conditions and stop at that. Successful mediation in the Middle East and the entire Arab region should be able to identify a particular style of mediation and work towards achieving success in it.

The four mediator styles are: Facilitative Mediation; Transformative Mediation; Evaluative Mediation; Restorative Justice Mediation. The first three were the original styles of mediation. Restorative Justice later became part of the group; it is described as "a systematic response to wrongdoing that emphasizes healing the wounds of victims, offenders and communities caused or revealed by the criminal behavior" (Chan).

The main point in Restorative Justice Mediation is identifying and taking steps to repair harm. Another focal point here is to identify the nature and extent of the victim's loss and to explore how the offender might begin to repair the harm caused by the criminal act. Yet another important aspect is that agreements are made concerning restitution schedules, follow-up meetings and monitoring procedures (Chan, VanNess, Strong).

Facilitative is the foremost style of mediation. In facilitative mediation, the mediator structures a process to assist the parties in reaching a mutually agreeable resolution.

One advantage of this style is that it empowers parties to take responsibility for their own dispute and the resolution of the dispute. The flip side of this style is that mediation takes too long, and too often ends without agreement (Zumeta, Chan).

Transformative mediation has similar advantages and disadvantages as facilitative mediation. Supporters of transformative mediation worry that outcomes can be contrary to standards of fairness and that mediators in these approaches cannot protect the weaker party. The distinctive points of transformative mediation are:

- Transformative mediators leave responsibility for the outcomes with the parties.
- Transformative mediators feel (and express) a sense of success when empowerment and recognition occur, even in small degrees. They do not see a lack of settlement as a failure (Zumeta, Chan, Spangler, Bush, Folger).

In evaluative mediation, the mediator controls the process and suggests solutions for resolving the conflict. The focus of an evaluative mediation is primarily upon settlement. The mediators will make their best efforts to get the parties to compromise, if necessary, to achieve a result (Chan, Zumeta).

Sometimes, the problem lies with the individuals who try to prove stubborn in mediation. At such times, a couple of strategies could be of assistance. If in the course of mediation the parties refuse to play or deliberately employ some deceptive dirty tricks, the mediation process might be jeopardized if not handled properly.

There are a couple of ways to get reluctant players to participate in mediation. You may yourself concentrate on the merits, rather than on position. In effect, you can change the game simply by starting a new one. Some of the methods include the following:

- Principled Negotiation
- Negotiation Jujitsu
- One-Text Procedure (Ury).

Of all the methods propounded by Ury, *One-text Procedure* seems to remain a formidable force to getting the other party participate effectively in reaching a negotiated settlement. The unique thing about this process is that through the instrumentality of a third party, a number of puzzles could be solved. For example, a third party can often suggest some impartial basis for resolving differences. He can separate the people from the problem and direct the discussion to interests and options.

A popular opinion is that *One-text Procedure* is comparable to *Shuttle Diplomacy* in mediation. In *One-text Procedure,* even if the other side is not willing to talk to you directly or vice versa, a third party can take a draft around. In *Shuttle Diplomacy,* the mediator practically oscillates between the disputants, same as in *One-text Procedure*. One disadvantage of *One-text Procedure* is the possibility of the other party to misrepresent facts and figures. A wise approach to forestall this negative probability is to separate the people from the problem. Another approach is not to take them for their word, unless absolutely convinced of their claim. It is only prudent, fair and safe to advance this approach if the physical surroundings seem to be prejudicial.

Positional Bargaining

There is a natural inclination for people to defend their claims and beliefs, irrespective of whatever any other party says, thinks or believes. However, there comes a point when someone has to yield to the other for peaceful and harmonious co-existence. This is a case where Positional Bargaining is shelved.

Positional Bargaining therefore, is a situation whereby people in a dispute stick to their own side of the story with little or no interest in, or consideration for the other party's story line. Each of the parties argues only to defend their position, with some concession just for the purpose of reaching a compromise. Studies have proven that such agreements attained through positional bargaining are so ephemeral, unreliable, unwise, inefficient, a waste of time and therefore, one easy way to lose face in relationships. As more attention is paid to positions, less attention is devoted to the underlying concerns of the parties. (Fisher, Patton, Ury).

The flip side of the futility of positional bargaining is what The Harvard Negotiation Project called *principled negotiation* or *negotiation on the merits*. The method is summarized as follows:

People: separate the people from the problem

Interests: focus on interests, not positions

Options: generate a variety of possibilities before deciding what to do

Criteria: insist that the result be based on some objective standard.

In contrast to positional bargaining, the principled negotiation method of focusing on basic interests, mutually satisfying options and fair standards typically results in a *wise* agreement (Ury).

It is absolutely important to note that it takes skill, intelligence and astuteness to be able to counter tricks and innuendos emitting from the opponent's camp. It is only he who is able to decipher the other party's mindset that succeeds in reaching a negotiated and possibly lasting agreement. It is equally worthy of note that the project of conflict resolution and de-escalation can only succeed when all parties in conflict are able to cooperate with mediators in an effort to reach a workable compromise.

EPILOGUE

My assessment of this work is that it has only scratched the surface of the complex issues in a complex subject matter. Dispute/conflict resolution and de-escalation within a particular region of the world – in this case, the Middle East and the Arab world or between individual members of a given locality, is as challenging as the topic itself. I make this assessment with the same humility, which propelled Thomas Aquinas to conclude, "All that I have written seems to me like straw compared to what has now been revealed to me" (Holt, 2008). However, given the scope of the work, I believe I have done a great job in stimulating academic discussions on the subject of *Dispute/conflict resolution and de-escalation* in the human family. The book is by no means an exhaustive discussion on the subject; it rather exposes new vistas for both the International community and mediators in general to address local and widespread conflicts before and after escalation.

The necessity of Dispute/conflict resolution and de-escalation cannot be over emphasized. We may not all live in a particular part of the world, but as a global village, an upheaval in one region of the world affects all other regions. The entire world should not fold their arms and wait for individuals and nations to resolve their own conflicts. The United Nations and other meaningful and peace-loving individuals and organizations must step in and facilitate conflict resolution and de-escalation efforts in our universe.

The ripple effects of wars and conflicts have no boundaries. For instance, the civil war between Nigeria and Biafra caused the influx of refugees in Gabon. The Liberia war caused a huge immigration of refugees in Nigeria. These countries have no geographical boundaries. The ongoing conflicts in Syria and Afghan are the major reason Turkey and other regional neighbors are saturated with fleeing refugees. Conflicts in the Middle East are capable, and have sent energy costs skyrocketing in major consumer nations.

Therefore, the whole human race must come together to mediate in conflicts before they escalate. These mediation efforts give rise to peaceful political transition, reduce recriminations emanating from conflicts, give rise to interpersonal harmony, and eventually result in socioeconomic prosperity in the world. It is with the power of conflict de-escalation that the world could forestall another *Arab Spring*, *Occupy* protests, *Black Lives Matter* protests and similar disputes around the globe.

RESOURCES AND BIBLIOGRAPHY

Books

Adichie, Chimamanda N. *Half of a Yellow Sun*. London: Harper Perennial, 2007.
Aguilera, Donna C. *Crisis Intervention: Theory and Methodology*. 8th ed. New York: Mosby, 1998.
Beer, Jennifer E. with Eileen Steif. *The Mediator's Hand Book*. Canada: New Society Publishers, 1997.
Bercovitch, Jacob. *Studies in International Mediation*, Palgrave Macmillan, New York 2003.
Carnegie, Dale, *How to Win Friends and Influence People*. Pocket Books, 1981
Chan, Henry A. *The Humanity of Mediators: From A Study of the Major Concepts of Viktor E. Frankl*. Lima, Ohio: Wyndham Hall Press, 2007.
Ehusani, George, *An Afro-Christian Vision "OZOVEHE!" Toward A More Humanized World*, (New York: University Press of America, 1991)
Frankl, Viktor E., *THE WILL TO MEANING Foundations And Applications Of Logotherapy*, New York, Meridian Press, 1988.
Griffee, Dale T., *Research Tips: Interview Data Collection*, Journal of Developmental Education, National Center for

Developmental Education, Appalachian State University, Boone, NC, 2005, p. 36

Gelvin, James L. *The Arab Uprisings*, what everyone needs to know. Oxford University Press. 2012

Hart, Michael. *The 100: A Ranking of the Most Influential Persons in History.* Citadel Press, 1992.

Hoffman, Bruce. *Inside Terrorism.* Columbia University Press, 2006

Hope, Mary Kendall. Iraq: *How Conflict Resolution Can Defeat Terrorism.*

Eloquent Books (2008).

Hugh, Miall, *Conflict Transformation: A Multi-Dimensional Task, Berghof Handbook for Conflict Transformation*, 2004.

Juhasz, Antonia. *The Bush Agenda: Invading the World, One Economy at a Time.*

HarperCollins Publishers, Inc. New York, 2006.

Nwachukwu, Anthony. Keeping Human Relationships Together: *Self Guide to Healthy Living [Studies in Spiritual Psychology vis-à-vis Human Values]*. Bloomington, *iUniverse Publishers*, 2010.

Sisk, D. Timothy. *Power sharing and international mediation in ethnic conflicts.* Carnegie Corp of NY. (1996).

Tylor, Edward B. *Primitive Culture,* 1871.

Ury, William. *Getting Past No: Negotiating with Difficult People.* (1991) New York: Random House.

Ury, et al. *Getting to Yes: Negotiating Agreements without Giving In* (1991) New York: Penguin Books.

Articles, Journals, Encyclopedias And Internet sources

A&E Television Networks, 2012
(ajami Fouad. *http://www.foreignaffairs.com/articles/137053/ fouad-ajami/the-arab-spring-at-one*. Retrieved April 22, 2012).
Arthur Schechter. *www.Schechtergroup.com*. Retrieved 04/19/12)
http://middleeast.about.com/od/yemen/p/ali-abdullah-saleh-profile.htm. Retrieved March 12, 2012.
http://history1900s.about.com/od/saddamhussein/p/saddamhussein.htm. Retrieved April 12, 2012
http://atheism.about.com/od/popejohnpaulii/a/iraqwar.htm. Retrieved May 1, 2012.
"African Culture" (AMHARA) accessed on February 5, 2011 from africaguide.com (2010)
AmericanCatholic.org.
café-Syria.com
Collins English Dictionary - Complete & Unabridged 10th Edition, 2009.
http://www.commondreams.org/headlines03/0321-02.htm. (Retrieved May 1, 2012).
"Conflict Management", (Conflict) Work911/Bacal & Associates Business & Management Supersite, accessed on February 05, 2011 from http://www.work911.com/conflict/index.htm, 2010.
Conflict Research Consortium, University of Colorado. (Accessed 12/2011).
David Stout, *The New York Times*, August 31, 2006
http://www.differencebetween.net/miscellaneous/difference-between-religion-and-spirituality (Retrieved April 29. 2012).
Conjecture Corporation, 2012.

Cultural Empathy (Empathize) accessed on 30 January 2011 from EmpatiaResolutions.com (2008).

"Definition of Culture", (Culture) accessed on 30 January 2011 from Roshan Cultural Heritage Institute (2001)

Eastern European, (Europe) *InternationalBusinessCenter.org*, (2007), accessed on February 5, 2011 from Mediate.com, 2010.

"Empathy in Mediation", (Empathy) accessed on 30 January 2011 from *faculty.mc3.edu*.

Encyclopedia of World Biography. 2005-2006

Encyclopedia of Mental Disorders

Faure and Zartman *Negotiating with Terrorists*, Strategy, Tactics, and Politics, 2010

http://www.foreignaffairs.com/author/jack-a-goldstone; Mar/Apr. 2012, Vol. 91 Issue 2.

Heidi Blake (ed). *The Telegraph*, 2011*Iran Chamber Society*, 2011

http://www.ivythesis.com/samples/ThesisPaper Methodology.htm.

http://www.jewishvirtuallibrary.org/jsource/biography/Mubarak.html. Retrieved March 12, 2012).

Larry Johnson, *noquarterusa.net/arab-spring-or-middle-east-firestorm/*. Retrieved April 5, 2012).

Mahmoud Ahmadinejad. (2012). http://www.biography.com/people/mahmoud-ahmadinejad-38656. (Retrieved 02:47, Jul 07, 2012).

Marc Lynch. *http//thebrowser.com/intervies/marc-lynch-on-Origins-of-the-Arab-Uprising*. Retrieved April 21, 2012).

Merriam-Webster's Dictionary of Law, 1996

mw1.meriam-webster.com

Oregon Mediation Center, Inc. 2011

http://www.philosophyofreligion.info/whos-who/historic-figures/st-thomas-aquinas/ (Retrieved 07/21/2012).

Rahim, M. A. (2002) Toward a theory of managing organizational conflict. The International Journal of Conflict Management, 13, 208.

rbenjamin.com. (Accessed 12/11/2011).

religion. (n.d.). *Dictionary.com Unabridged*. Retrieved July 17, 2012, from Dictionary.com website: http://dictionary.reference.com/browse/religion

Richelson, (ed.) *National Security Archive*. 2011

Robinson., *Ontario Consultants on Religious Tolerance*, 2011

Sgubini, Alessandra. Mediation and Culture: How different cultural backgrounds can affect the way people negotiate and resolve disputes. Mediate.com . 2011.

Suzanne Goldenberg (ed). *The Guardian*, 2011

The *Department of Veterans Affairs, Office Of The Dispute Resolution Specialist* (Accessed 12/11/2011).

The Harvard Negotiation Project (Accessed 01/12/2012)

The New Jerusalem Bible

The New York Times Company, 2006

The President and Fellows of Harvard College (2010).

The U.S. and the Middle East Since 1945, A Guide to Mideast Policy from Harry Truman to George W. Bush. http//About.com/middleeast. Retrieved 04/19/12.)

William, Saletan, The Slate Group, a Division of the Washington Post Company. http://www.slate.com/articles/technology/future_tense/2011/07/springtime_for_twitter.html

Zumeta, Zena, *Styles Of Mediation* Mediate.Com. (2000).

www.ingramcontent.com/pod-product-compliance
Ingram Content Group UK Ltd.
Pitfield, Milton Keynes, MK11 3LW, UK
UKHW022214230426
12048UKWH00016BA/844